MONASTIC WISDOM SERIES: NUMBER TEN

Elizabeth Connor, ocso

Charles Dumont: Monk-Poet

A Spiritual Biography

MONASTIC WISDOM SERIES

MW1 Cassian and the Fathers: Initiation into the Monastic Tradition
Thomas Merton, OCSO

MW2 Secret of the Heart: Spiritual Being
Jean-Marie Howe, OCSO

MW3 Inside the Psalms: Reflections for Novices
Maureen F. McCabe, OCSO

MW4 Thomas Merton: Prophet of Renewal
John Eudes Bamberger, OCSO

MW5 Centered on Christ: A Guide to Monastic Profession
Augustine Roberts, OCSO

MW6 Passing from Self to God: A Cistercian Retreat
Robert Thomas, OCSO

MW7 Dom Gabriel Sortais: An Amazing Abbot in Turbulent Times
Guy Oury, OSB

MW8 A Monastic Vision for the 21st Century: Where Do We Go from Here?
Patrick Hart, OCSO, editor

MW9 Pre-Benedictine Monasticism: Initiation into the Monastic Tradition 2
Thomas Merton, OCSO

MW10 Charles Dumont: Monk-Poet A Spiritual Biography
Elizabeth Connor, OCSO

MW11 The Way of Humility
André Louf, OCSO

Cistercian Publications
Editorial Offices
The Institute of Cistercian Studies
Western Michigan University
Kalamazoo, Michigan 49008-5415
cistpub@wmich.edu

The work of Cistercian Publications is made possible in part by support from Western Michigan University to The Institute of Cistercian Studies.

Library of Congress Cataloging-in-Publication Data

Connor, Elizabeth.
Charles Dumont, monk-poet : a spiritual biography / by Elizabeth Connor ; foreword by Mark A. Scott.
p. cm. — (Monastic wisdom series ; no. 10)
Includes index.
ISBN-13: 978-0-87907-040-3
ISBN-10: 0-87907-040-4
1. Dumont, Charles. 2. Trappists—Biography. 3. Cistercians—Biography. I. Title. II. Series.

BX4705.D868C66 2007
271'.1202—dc22
[B]

2007008239

Printed in the United States of America

MONASTIC WISDOM SERIES: NUMBER TEN

Charles Dumont: Monk-Poet

A Spiritual Biography

by

Elizabeth Connor, OCSO

Foreword by

Mark A. Scott, OCSO

CISTERCIAN PUBLICATIONS
Kalamazoo, Michigan

CONTENTS

FOREWORD

Fr. Charles Dumont was "present at the creation." As this enlightening book shows, Fr. Charles' life as a man, a Christian, a monk, a friend, an artist, and a scholar, has not only coincided with but also, providentially, largely informed the beginning of a new era for the Order of Cistercians of the Strict Observance. Fr. Charles was part of that "renaissance" that contributed the minds and materials for Vatican Council II and the subsequent renewal of Cistercian life and Constitutions. In addition, Fr. Charles has been a major player in making sure that there have been resources and energy enough for the momentum of renewal to continue.

With his unique grasp of the inexhaustible Cistercian tradition and his special gift of friendship, Fr. Charles has been directly instrumental in disclosing to three generations of monks and nuns unsuspected possibilities contained in the Cistercian patrimony. He has followed through with that disclosure by confidently guiding them into this new terrain. The published collections of Fr. Charles' essays, and his unmatched book *Pathway of Peace,*[1] assure that Fr. Charles' influence will continue upon succeeding generations of Cistercians, both professed and lay. Sr. Elizabeth Connor's book is a deserved and timely tribute to this outstanding figure in Cistercian history.

Fr. Charles' life, spanning almost the entire twentieth century and into the twenty-first, is situated in a world that many reading this book will have been a part of.

1. Charles Dumont, *Pathway of Peace. Cistercian Wisdom according to Saint Bernard.* Trans. Elizabeth Connor, ocso. Cistercian Studies Series 187 (Kalamazoo: Cistercian Publications, 1999).

This very same world spun differently is the setting for the life of Fr. Charles' friend and contemporary Thomas Merton. Spun another, it is the world of his early confrere Fr. Francis Acharya and of his colleague in scholarship Edmund Mikkers. Tilted somewhat to the south, it is, in its earlier decades, the world of Blessed Rafael Arnáiz Barón, Fr. Charles' senior by only seven years, and of Blessed Maria Gabriella Sagheddu, his senior by four. Spun in other ways still, it is the world of Ambrose Southey and of Thomas Keating, of Jean-Marie Howe and Hortense Berthet.

In some part, finally, the world of Fr. Charles is the world that those of us thirty and forty and fifty years younger than he find ourselves co-heirs to. It is the common setting out of which the lives that we ourselves uniquely are emerged and which we carry forward. In all cases, it is the story of grace, of "eternity in time."

In 1995, Fr. Charles said in a homily: "The life of a monk is a sprint toward the infinity of God. The whole effort of the spiritual life comes down to living in the present with wisdom, reflecting on our past with sorrow in our soul, and preparing our future with patience and perseverance . . . Such unification of time already gives it an aura of eternity" (Chapter 6, p. 145). There are traces here of Saint Bernard's three "faculties of the soul," memory, understanding, and will. "Living with wisdom" is Bernard's understanding, "reflection on the past" is memory, and preparing for the future in such a way as to effect a synthesis in one's own life of time and eternity, is the function, for Bernard, of the human will. Fr. Charles probably did not have that "little trinity" in mind when he wrote his homily, making the fact of the traces all the more significant.

In Fr. Charles' case, it is in his life as poet that *memory* has been most at play. As every poet does, Fr. Charles has created his personal world by shaping the contents of his consciousness, his "memory," into his "poems, prayers and songs." Sr. Elizabeth tells us that Fr. Charles remembered the occasion of every poem he wrote, though he had the habit of not rereading his own poetry. Fr. Charles himself says, "It is in my poems that I recognize myself best . . . Really, my whole life is in them" (Chapter 7, pp. 163–164).

As for the role of *understanding* in his life, we have only to look at Fr. Charles' lifelong devotion to monastic scholarship, to teaching and mentoring, and, beneath both of those, to the practice of monastic *lectio divina.* Fr. Charles found intellectual kinship with the great names of European existentialism and phenomenology. Some would not agree with all of Fr. Charles' intellectual enthusiasms. For instance, we learn that Fr. Charles felt an increasing affinity with Emmanuel Levinas. For the American Orthodox theologian David Bentley Hart, Levinas' thought is a "prodigy of incoherence." And while admitting that Levinas' work presently enjoys a good opinion, Hart contends that it is "poor philosophy—the banal tortured into counterfeit profundity, the obviously false propounded as irresistibly true." In Hart's opinion, the view of the world Levinas advances is "perhaps a little depraved."[2] Fr. Charles saw things differently, and who is to say if he, or Hart, has the better understanding? Fr. Charles, in any case, with his broad grasp of culture and intellectual history, has been able convincingly and intelligently to explain the world of the twelfth century through the eyes of the twentieth.

Finally, Saint Bernard's *will* takes shape in Fr. Charles' desire for "true and eternal life" (RB Pro 17). It becomes clear from Sr. Elizabeth's delicate narrative that Fr. Charles' exercise of *will* in this direction was the force of his life. When he was not yet nine years old, Charles' mother Marguerite died. "The enigma of death," we are told, "and the life beyond captured his mind to the point that the mystery of time and eternity occupied a predominant and essential place in his spiritual reflection for the rest of his life" (Ch. 1, p. 3). In a sense, this book is simply the narration of the contours of Fr. Charles' reflection upon this mystery over the next eighty years. I hazard to guess that Fr. Charles would find something of his own echoed in this poem of his older contemporary Pablo Neruda:

2. David Bentley Hart, *The Beauty of the Infinite: The Aesthetics of Christian Truth* (Grand Rapids: 2003) 75.

> Ah, let what I am go on existing and ceasing to exist
> and let my obedience be ordered with such iron conditions
> that the tremor of deaths and of births will not trouble
> the deep place that I wish to keep for myself eternally.
> Let what I am, then, be, in some place and in every time,
> an established and assured and ardent witness,
> carefully destroying himself and preserving himself
> incessantly,
> clearly insistent upon his original duty.[3]

When, at twenty-three, Charles Dumont entered Scourmont in 1941, the Spanish Trappist oblate Rafael Arnáiz Barón had been dead three years already. If the world had spun a different way for Br. Rafael, he would be ninety-five years old today, not an unlikely age for a monk. In many particulars, both Rafael and Charles lived in the same Catholic world and entered into the same Trappist culture. Furthermore, Br. Rafael, like Fr. Charles, was chronically ill. And like Fr. Charles, Br. Rafael had a spirituality of yearning. "*Saber esperar,*" he would say, "Know how to wait, how to hope."

But how different Br. Rafael's perspective was from Fr. Charles'. "When the spirit loses itself in the thought of eternity," Br. Rafael wrote when he was twenty-five, "what interest can it take in the short and limited time of its life? When the heart yearns for the heavenly homeland and its union with the Eternal, with what indifference will it not see this valley of tears? . . . In those moments, you forget the world, so damaged and small . . . You forget people caught up in their concerns, their struggles, their misfortunes. The soul suffers for being still on earth . . . How is it possible to love this life when it is the very thing that separates us from God?"[4]

For his part, Fr. Charles, in his twenty-ninth year, wrote to his grandmother, "I imagine that God measures our love, and

3. Pablo Neruda, "It Means Shadows." (*Significa Sombras*) in Pablo Neruda, *Residence on Earth,* Bilingual edition, trans. Donald D. Walsh (New York: 2004) 93.

4. Rafael Arnáiz Barón, *Obras Completas,* 4th edition (Burgos: 2002) 641, 642, my translation.

therefore the place we will have near Him (in heaven) by our desire. We have to desire heaven above all else . . . But then Saint Paul thought of the faithful who needed him. As long as there is good to do, happiness to give, life is beautiful and desirable" (Chapter 2, p. 15). Nearly fifty years later, Fr. Charles will say: "I live the resurrection already. To arrive at the resurrection, a person must have a deep knowledge of Christ . . . This makes all the difference. It gives meaning to my human sufferings, to my life and to my death" (Chapter 6, p. 146). Perhaps Fr. Charles' "final poem," *L'épreuve d'aimer,* expresses his difference from Br. Rafael best of all:

> Life is to think of as a test
> — A road to travel in given time —
> . . .
> If the road is monotonous and gray
> Take pleasure then in walking;
> If your peace, as you go, amazes you
> You will know the happiness of seeking. (Chapter 7, p. 173)

The example of Br. Rafael is useful. If the Trappist worlds of Rafael in Spain and Charles in Belgium were parallel in many respects, still, Rafael did not have, as Charles did, a Dom Anselme Le Bail. Rafael did not have at San Isidro the prodigious ensemble of scholar-monks that Charles did at Scourmont to introduce him to the intellectual and spiritual possibilities in the Cistercian patrimony, in the critical study of Scripture, and in theology and spirituality.

More to the point, if the world had turned differently for Rafael, he undoubtedly would have come into contact with Fr. Charles the scholar and teacher, mentor and friend who would have enriched Rafael's native spiritual sensitivity with the addition of Cistercian horizons and biblical depth. True to the spirituality he had at hand, Rafael awaited release and complete "separation." Fr. Charles, by contrast, strives for "synthesis."

Synthesis is a word that occurs over and over again in Sr. Elizabeth's account, especially in the later chapters. As a

Cistercian *scholar,* the synthesis Fr. Charles was always working towards was the one he finally achieved with his book on Saint Bernard, *Pathway of Peace.*

Another recurring word is "friendship," and for Fr. Charles friendship has been another synthesis achieved, the synthesis of "I" and "Thou," of undeniable and sometimes painful solitude and honest human affection. There is also the synthesis of artist and community member, poet and scholar, a synthesis Fr. Charles has achieved imperfectly, but perhaps better than Thomas Merton, his companion across the Atlantic, had. There are the syntheses of academic labor and mysticism, of the traveling teacher and the restful contemplative, of twentieth-century existentialism and twelfth-century Christian anthropology, of patience in infirmity and self-possessed independence. As a Cistercian *monk,* finally, there is for Fr. Charles the synthesis called "eternity in time," "resurrection now." As Saint Aelred, Fr. Charles' lifelong Cistercian master, said, Easter is the eighth day on which the Creator put heaven and earth together. "In it there is only eternity and stability . . . This day has started now, because the resurrection has begun."[5]

The author of this book, as will become clear, was uniquely qualified to write it. She has been associated with Fr. Charles as coworker, translator and friend. Contemporary and future Cistercians, lay and professed, owe a great deal to Sr. Elizabeth Connor for this fine book.

Mark A. Scott, ocso
Assumption Abbey, Ava

5. Aelred of Rievaulx, *Sermon 41 for Easter Day,* in *Sermons pour l'année* 3: Deuxième collection de Clairvaux. Intro Pierre-André Burton, trans. Gaëtane de Briey. Pain de Cîteaux, 3e série 18 (Oka: Abbaye N.-D. du Lac, 2002) 162, my translation.

1

CHILDHOOD AND YOUTH

We have come to know and believe in the love God has for us.

1 John 4:16

On September 26, 1918, in Ixelles, a district of Brussels first mentioned in documents dating from the thirteenth century, a son was born to Émile and Marguerite Dumont. The First World War which had dragged on for so long was at last nearing its end. The new baby, his parents' first child, was baptized in the church of St. Boniface hardly more than a stone's throw from their home and was given the name of Charles Émile Pierre Maurice. The very day of Charles' birth the gigantic allied Meuse-Argonne attack began, opening the way to an Armistice, so that the family endearingly dubbed him the "Angel of Victory." A fragile angel indeed, as fragile as the peace that ended the hostilities. Scarcely had little Charles seen the light of day when he almost died of an intestinal disorder. Poor health, in fact, was to be his almost constant companion during his whole life. Two little girls, Francine (1922) and Nicole (1924), came after to complete the closely-knit Dumont family.

Émile Dumont and his wife Marguerite Cuyle grew up in two neighboring towns very close to the French-Belgian border. Marguerite, who was Flemish, lived in Menin. Émile, who had been born in Brussels, resided in Halluin. His father was in the textile business for which the region had been renowned for centuries. Émile worked with him for a while, then moved to Brussels where he became the director of a tailoring establishment. When Charles was four years old, Monsieur Dumont's health required a change of air so the family moved temporarily to Genval, in Brabant, not far from Waterloo. At Genval Charles was with his mother almost constantly. Madame Dumont saw to her son's schooling herself, so that the affective bond that existed between them became even stronger. There was a lake near their home. Its calm waters made a deep impression on the small child whose reflective and poetic nature had already begun to reveal itself. This period of peaceful happiness left images deeply graven in his memory. Long after he spoke of them in a poem about his mother. Here two stanzas of it are quoted:

> In the slowing season of autumn when ripe fruit falls
> I went again to see the lake where my childhood still lingered
> On the paths of long ago along the walls,
> The water did not remember.
>
> . . . .
>
> Dreaming of her where my image floated on the water,
> In the moving reflections of the sky now more star strewn
> I thought I saw your smile, O mother, and your face
> And your gestures so closely bound to mine.[1]

In autumn, 1926, the family returned to Brussels and took up residence in the Woluwe Saint Pierre section, near the Jesuit College of Saint Michel. Charles entered Saint Michel as a 10th form student; he was eight years old. A few months later, on March 7, 1927, Marguerite died very unexpectedly after an operation. Suddenly she was no longer there. Questions invaded the child's mind: Where had his mother gone? Where was she? He returned again and again to the silent rooms where they had so often been

* Translations from French of letters, poems, and other unpublished writings of Fr. Charles are by the author, unless otherwise indicated.

1. Charles Dumont, ocso, *"Mère!"* (stanzas 1 & 3) in *Poèmes et Prières*. Cahiers Scourmontois 2 (Scourmont: 2000) 58.

together, hoping to detect her presence. This early experience of grief and loss was to have a deep effect on Charles. His mother is very present in his poetry, and the enigma of death and the life beyond captured his mind to the point that the mystery of time and eternity has occupied a predominant and essential place in his spiritual reflection during his whole life.

After Mrs. Dumont's death, Charles' paternal grandmother took over raising the family, encircling the children with warm affection and gentleness. During his school years at Saint Michel Charles excelled especially in subjects related to French literature and language. He was an avid reader, and writing both prose and poetry came naturally to him. He also prepared sermons which he preached to his little sisters, attentive listeners. As a Boy Scout he participated in all the activities of his troop and met boys who became life-long friends. A photo taken during a camping weekend shows him in a clearing in the woods near Orval, perched on a tree branch and laughing while two other scouts labored to get a campfire going. On another camping trip he went to a rural place near Scourmont, but at that time he was not even aware that there was a monastery close by.

In 1934, at the end of 4th form (Greek-Latin), Charles left Saint Michel and took a course in tailoring as preparation for entering his father's business. Skills he acquired at this time were useful to him later on when he worked in the tailor shop at Scourmont. In view of his work Monsieur Dumont also sent him for a while to Leicester, England, to learn English. Once again he was almost in the shadow of a Cistercian monastery—this time Mount Saint Bernard's—without knowing it. The next year Charles participated in a retreat. Though later on in life he said that he had felt called to the priesthood since he was twelve years old, he was so repelled by the pressure put on him by the retreat master that he left abruptly in the middle of the week and went back to work with his father. About the same time he was busy with Cub Scouts, first as an assistant, then as den leader in Brussels. But God's call was still there. In 1936 he made another retreat, this time at Scourmont, without however taking any steps to enter the monastery.

Military Service

When Charles was nineteen, in February, 1938, he was called up for military service. For him that meant being assigned to the cyclist-riflemen (*carabiniers cyclistes*). He was stationed first at Tervuren, then at Spa where he broke his collar-bone in a sports match and landed up in the Military Hospital in Liege for a month. In a letter written on a scrap of paper on July 4, he gave his grandmother news of himself and at the same time shared some of his reflections with her. In these few lines we can see the nascent philosopher. The topics which preoccupied him at nineteen were to come up time and again in his later writings as a monk:

> . . . Prayer is irresistible and God does not refuse his grace to souls of good will. What people of our hectic and unstable world need are belief, hope and a promise of another life to believe in. Then their immediate interests would seem much less essential to them. Pascal said that a man cries with rage for eight days because he has lost his job, but cares little about providing for his eternity. There I go, philosophizing like a parish priest! Forgive me for this little bent I have, and be sure that I am still like I used to be. Balance! that is what my motto could be. It is the hallmark of the perfect man, *which I don't pretend to be!!* I spend some nice moments in the chapel . . . The army is a very serious stage in a man's life. One understands better the advantages of a family, a job, and freedom. Freedom, too underestimated by those who possess it, is the most precious thing a man can have. It is liberty which prods him on, but it is a double-edged sword. (7.4.38)

That summer while still recuperating from his accident he spent some time in army camp. One day his group of soldiers organized a visit to the Abbey at Achel in Holland, just across the border from where they were. Charles was not interested and stayed at headquarters. Not long after, in September, Hitler seized Austria and dismembered Czechoslovakia. For the time being Belgium did not seem to be threatened by war, but by August, 1939, it was evident that the situation was very precarious. Charles was sent to Gedinne, Houdremont, near the Belgian-French border. There he and another young soldier were sentinels for their company, with orders to give the alert if and when there would be an invasion across the French border. This assignment lasted until winter. During these months of solitude and silence in the forest of Croix-Scaille, steeped in the emptiness of waiting, the young soldier had ample time to read and reflect. He was still reading Pascal, from a copy of the *Pensées* given to him by a girl he had been dating. Reminiscing about this many years later he sighed with pity, "The poor girl!" Little did she know that Pascal would play a part in his vocation.

During the winter of 1939–1940 until the beginning of March Charles' regiment was stationed at Mons, then moved east to Neerpelt near the Dutch border in Limburg. One day, after watching the ripples in the wake of a barge gliding by in the Neerpelt canal, he went into a bomb shelter and with thoughts of his vocation on his mind wrote a poem which he entitled simply: "Far away" ("*Loin*"):

Au remous du chenal	On the ripples of the canal
Flottait la nostalgie	Floated nostalgia
D'un bonheur moins banal	Of happiness less banal
Que l'exacte magie	Than the exact magic
Des sigles connaissables	Of recognizable signs
Par trop bien attestés	Too well attested
Graffiti sur la sable	Graffiti on the sand
Aux berges répétés	Reflected on the banks
J'ai choisi l'eau profonde	I chose deep water
Préféré l'inconnu	Preferred the unknown
Seul et si loin du monde	Alone and so far from the world
Oublieux, calme et nu.	Forgetful, calm and without disguise.[2]

2. Fr. Charles reworked this poem at Jolimont twenty-five years later. He recognized that "everything is there already; my vocation is there." Cf. C. Dumont, *Poèmes et Prières,* 12.

While he was stationed in Neerpelt Charles attended a liturgical Office in the quiet convent chapel of the cloistered Daughters of the Cross, prayed in the parish church and read François Mauriac's *Life of Jesus* which touched him deeply and made him increasingly sure that God was calling him. Toward the end of March in a letter to his father he told him of his decision to enter the religious life. Monsieur Dumont was disconcerted, because he had counted on Charles to take over the family business in the future, but he was not completely surprised and replied by a letter that was "magnificent by its abnegation and comprehension."

It was at Neerpelt, on the tenth of May at 2 o'clock in the morning, that Charles heard the alert of the enemy attack . . . During the following "eighteen-day war, " he was continually in the thick of battle. Thanks to hastily jotted down notes—sometimes almost hour by hour—one can closely follow the action of his regiment. He lived through deafening bombardments, was at times in the first line of combat—once uninterruptedly for thirty-six hours—, had a close brush with death when a bullet hit his shovel clipped on his belt and knew moments of both terror and ghostly calm. But there were other moments, too, as when he pedaled with the retreating troops during one entire night under the velvet depths of the sky forming a canopy resplendent with stars. "The peace and joy before the torment. The joy of being a Christian, of believing in eternal life . . . We live as one ought to live, ready to leave, to leave everything" (5.21.40). He recited Compline for the first time, using a prayer book given to him by a sister at Wetteren.

After the surrender of the Belgian forces on May 28, 1940, Charles experienced the humiliation of being taken prisoner. There was however one small compensation: the German commanding officer complimented the survivors for their valor in battle. Fortunately, Charles' time of captivity lasted only a few days. On June 8 he was able to return to civilian life in Brussels where he resumed work with his father and his activities with the Cub Scouts. At the den meetings he took some time each week to read to the boys. One of the passages he chose was "The Miracle of Purun Bhagat" from Kipling's *Second Jungle Book.* The cubs listened avidly to the story of the distinguished Brahmin who left everything to become a hermit in a small deserted shrine high in the Himalayas. During this period Charles also belonged to a clandestine group who helped British aviators grounded behind enemy lines escape to Spain. Although he was aware of the danger he hid one of them in the Cub Scout meeting place, telling the boys confidentially: "Let's pretend he is a British aviator hiding here. So we mustn't say a word about it to *anyone!*" The boys, of course, were thrilled about playing this game and the aviator was safe as long as he remained in the city.

The war changed Charles. Seeing men die, some of them with great fervor and strong hope in eternal life, made him sure he wanted to become a monk. The next winter, preoccupied with thoughts of his vocation and vacillating painfully between grace and free choice, he spent several weeks at the Franciscan novitiate near Namur. He had always been attracted to the spirituality of St. Francis of Assisi, quite probably because like St. Francis he also was a poet, but the type of life he found in this novitiate was not what he was seeking and he did not stay. Soon after Charles wrote to Fr. Albert Derzelle, novice master of the Cistercian Trappist community of Scourmont, near Chimay. Fr. Albert encouraged him, and after a short retreat at the abbey Charles entered the monastery as a postulant on June 11, 1941. There he did find what he was seeking; he was sure that it was *there* that he should be. In later years, when asked why he chose to apply at Scourmont, he was likely to reply with a little smile: "Because there was no train for Orval." And that could well be the real reason. Providence often works in very simple, disarming and imponderable ways.[3] He described his sentiments on the day he entered:

3. In their book *L'appel de Dieu* (Paris: Cerf, 1982) 178–183, Jacques and Yvette Antier tell of how, the night before Charles left for the monastery, he and his father could hear each other walking back and forth in their rooms. Neither of them could bring himself to approach the other. Further on in this account it

Vocation

It was time to decide . . . to say goodbye: sad kisses, bonds of flesh, stifled sobs, and this heart which tightened up, this throat so dry, and energy melting away before this choice which could still be refused, like when someone nods "no," or when a man swims out from shore and then turns back . . . Was it really necessary?

If anyone wants to (Mt 16:24), Christ said to the young man. Freedom to choose, but grace was clear even though there was no way around it; like a gentle slope to which one simply needs to consent.

The sun was warm and golden on the countryside that day. Everything was calm and seemed easy. The earth was peaceful, as though it would be like that forever. Was it really necessary to tear myself away from this familiar horizon?

I had to leave: the trains go on time. And the rails threaded their way through this happy countryside. Setting out upon what kind of an adventure? Having to start again from scratch in a completely new life.

So he really had left: irresistible call, free response! It was done: he had made his choice and his gesture would remain recorded for eternity.

Like someone who decides some fine morning that it is time to reap, and one can already hear the swish of scythes at the base of the stalks of the ripe wheat. The choice had been made, finally; he had left everything. He had put his hand on the plow. "Whoever puts his hand on the plow. . . ." (Lc 9:62)

He had committed his whole existence to a furrow, and under the cutting sweep of steel an opaque, heavy world opened up to the warm and soft light of that morning.

---

is said that Charles entered Scourmont twice and that the first time the work on the farm and in the garden, for which he was in no way prepared, frightened him so much that he left. It should be pointed out that this did not occur after he entered as a postulant, but rather during a visit to the monastery prior to his entry. As he later said, "Memories blend together and become legend."

What struck him most when he entered the monastery was that he did so with complete freedom. Irresistible call, free response. He could have said "no."

Many years later, reflecting on this, he wrote: "I had the experience—unique in my life—of a moment of absolute freedom. Paradoxically, afterwards I could say that it was linked to the equally clear experience of the fact that I could not do otherwise."[4]

4. C. Dumont, unpublished.

2

SETTING OUT ON THE PATHWAY OF PEACE

Do what you love.
Dom Anselme Le Bail

Scourmont

Saint Joseph's Abbey at Scourmont was founded in 1850 by monks from Saint-Sixte Abbey in west Flanders. In 1941, when Charles entered the monastery, Dom Anselme Le Bail had been abbot for twenty-seven years. The community numbered over eighty monks, approximately half of whom had been mobilized while Belgium was at war. By June, 1941, however, most of them had returned to the monastery. It was a very difficult and challenging time to begin living the Trappist life, especially for a young man with frail health. War time penury was added to the regular austerity of the Rule.

Dom Anselme Le Bail was one of the most outstanding personalities of the monastic world in the twentieth century. Born in Morbihan, Brittany, on the last day of 1878, he entered Scourmont in 1904 and after serving the community as novice master and prior was elected abbot in 1913, at 34 years of age. Dom Anselme had great vision and love for the monastic life; he left an indelible mark on Scourmont. He used to say, "I want monks who are first of all men," and he saw to their formation accordingly. In a period when an ethos of austerity and work left over from the eighteenth century still prevailed in Trappist monasteries,

Dom Anselme's ways were often looked upon with suspicion and askance by his fellow abbots, but this did not bother him. He gave a very important place to study in his monks' lives, the kind of study which predisposes a monk to *lectio divina* and is integrally bound to the spiritual life. While he was abbot he sent nineteen monks to study in universities. Profiting from the severe restrictions on travel during the war, he set a precedent by sending some of his monks to Louvain, whereas the practice in the Order was to send students to Roman universities. Fr. Maur Standaert was the first Scourmont monk to study theology at Louvain and earn a doctorate there.

Dom Anselme's way of governing was summed up well in Scourmont's 1950 centennial booklet:

> From a spiritual point of view, Dom Anselme's years as abbot were characterized by the following traits: a return to Benedictine and Cistercian spirituality by the teaching of the Rule of Saint Benedict which is a veritable handbook of spirituality; the study of Cistercian spirituality; a more human conception of monastic formation and the establishment of a program of studies in conformity with this conception; the privileged place given to Cistercian studies in spirituality, liturgy, law and history; the organization of a monastic library adapted to these various goals; formation of a qualified group of monk-professors; an appeal to personal responsibility; and respect for each one's personality united to a spirit of both dependence and encouragement of individual initiative.[1]

As it happened, when Charles entered the monastery there were a number of very gifted monks in the Scourmont community, men competent in various fields of Cistercian and monastic studies: in theology Fr. Thomas Litt, whose brother was vice-rector of the University of Louvain; the prodigious Fr. Gall

1. Columban Bock, OCR, *Scourmont* 1850–1950. *Un siècle de vie monastique.* Chapter 2. "Un siècle d'histoire de Scourmont" (Forges–lez–Chimay: Scourmont, 1950) 55.

who gave his lectures in Holy Scripture using only a Hebrew Bible; Frs. Colomban Bock and Joseph Canivez in Canon Law; Fr. Camille Hontoir in spirituality; and among the younger monks, Fr. Maur Standaert and Fr. Corneille Halflants in Cistercian studies; Fr. Robert Pourtoit who specialized in the writings of Cardinal Newman; and Fr. Francis Mahieu who later became the founder of Kurisumala in India. Dom Godefroid Bélorgey, who was Dom Anselme's prior before he became auxiliary Abbot of Cîteaux, and Fr. Albert Derzelle, the novice master, worked hand in hand with their abbot to maintain the tone and goals of the community. There were also holy lay brothers such as Br. Théophile whom Charles revered and for whom, after his death, he wrote a poem.[2] But it was above all Dom Anselme who, by his daily chapter talks and conferences, communicated his enthusiasm and love for the Rule and the Cistercian Fathers to the community as a whole, and to the individual monks by his personal relationship with each one. As one monk remarked many years later, "Dom Anselme made each one feel that it was he that he loved most."

It was in this atmosphere, one of wartime austerity and insecurity but also of monastic enthusiasm, that Charles found himself when he entered Scourmont. On the feast of the Visitation, July 2, 1941, he was clothed with the habit and became a novice. Charles's father, present on this occasion, afterwards wrote to his son: "I am happy for you, and for me, too, to see that you are a man, master of your destiny, and that you know what you want and what you love." This rather astonishing last phrase was an echo of words spoken by Dom Anselme at Br. Charles' clothing ceremony, when he told him to make his decision but to do what he loved. Could it be stated any better?

The new novice's love for his vocation grew. The great adventure of his Cistercian life had begun. He was introduced to the teachings of Saint Bernard and Saint Aelred, followed the

2. Fr. Charles said later that it was from Br. Théophile that he learned how to suffer.

regular novitiate program and felt increasingly at home in the community.

Momignies

Still, outside the monastery the war continued. On April 12, 1942, a Luftwaffe unit arrived at Scourmont to set up a radar post on the monks' property for sound-tracking aircraft. The monks, expelled from their monastery, took refuge provisionally in outbuildings of the Château in Chimay, before moving on to the Christian Brothers' Saint Jean-Baptiste de la Salle School at Momignies, about twelve miles from Scourmont. This situation lasted twenty-eight months.

During this whole period at Momignies the Abbot saw to it that the liturgy was celebrated as usual. He kept his community united, gave his regular chapter talks to the monks, and in spite of the heavy work load necessary for survival saw to it that careful attention was given to the juniors' formation. Business as usual, or at least as nearly usual as possible. It was in the chapel at Momignies, on July 2, 1943, that Charles made his first vows as a Cistercian. It was there also that he had a fleeting spiritual experience which marked his whole life.[3]

The Gestapo kept an eye on the monks and sometimes paid them unexpected visits. It was on those days especially that each of the monks realized how fragile his life was. On the morning of December 9, 1943, while most of the monks were occupied with their *lectio divina,* armed SS troopers appeared at the door. After searching the building they made the monks line up before them in the school's would-be cloister. Nine of the monks were notified that they were going to be taken to Saint-Gilles prison in Brussels. Not knowing what the future would bring, Fr. Thomas Litt, who was among those called, caught Br. Charles' eye and risked whispering to him that his notes for his course on logic were in his desk. The Gestapo intended to take Dom Anselme, but Fr. Albert Derzelle was able to convince them that the abbot's

3. See C. Dumont, "À quatre-vingt ans," *Poèmes et Prières,* 128.

presence was necessary for the community, and he himself offered to go in his place. Immediately after the hasty departure of the arrested monks Dom Anselme began to employ every possible strategy to obtain their release. By February 15, 1944, all were back at Momignies, except Fr. Albert who was released a month later.

American troops crossed the Belgian border near Momignies on September 2, 1944. Liberation! Like everyone else, the monks were caught up in the tremendous wave of euphoria of at last being free again. The very same day Dom Anselme went back to Scourmont with several of the monks to see what condition the monastery was in. As soon as the community was able to return to the abbey they set about cleaning up the pillaged buildings and cultivating the land. Unfortunately, they discovered that there were still plenty of Germans around. There was even another surprise visit from the Gestapo. Fr. Charles has vivid memories of that day. The very young SS troopers, almost boys, marched solemnly through the cloisters, holding high a portrait of Hitler ("like in a Blessed Sacrament procession," Fr. Charles says when telling this story), while the monks stood there looking on. It was a tense moment for everyone. Finally, the soldiers left.

The years immediately following the war were characterized by great austerity. The community's resources were depleted and restoring the monastery was an immense task. Nevertheless, the monastic life continued normally. While continuing his studies Br. Charles worked in the tailor shop, an occupation more suited to his physical capacities than work in the fields, but he also helped to plant the forest across the road in front of the monastery, which is still there today.

On July 16, 1946, the feast of Saint Stephen Harding, Br. Charles made solemn profession. The evening before, Fr. Albert wrote him the following note:

> I know that you want your offering to be complete: because of that be in security, peace and joy. Banish all hesitations

> and explanations; from now on all that is just temptation. I believe that you are in the type of life which is right for you and will assure your spiritual and human development . . . at what price? Suffering and the cross. Since Christ there is no other way.[4]

The next spring, in his Easter letter to his grandmother, the young monk wrote to her about heaven:

> I imagine that God measures our love, and therefore the place we will have near Him (in heaven), by our desire. We have to desire heaven above all else and, with Saint Paul, desire to die so that we may be with Christ. But then Saint Paul thought about the faithful who needed him. As long as there is good to do, happiness to give, life is beautiful and desirable. And even if we were all alone, by ourselves, abandoned, there would still be this beautiful praise to sing: that is, to do God's will. This human praise is unique; it has a very special value. The angels sing God's glory with all their might, but they see God so it is easy. We are behind the veil, living in faith, and that is why a human being's piety, praise and adoration have a very special significance which God loves. (4.14.47)

Once again, we can see that eternity occupied Charles' mind and spirit. On December 3 of that year Monsieur Dumont died. Putting aside his own devastating sorrow, the young monk did all he could to console and encourage his grandmother and two younger sisters in their bereavement. To his grandmother he wrote: "I liked to remind Papa that he was a bit of a 'monk' with me because he had actively participated in my sacrifice, and because he was united to my life by his generous consent to it" (12.20.47).

This whole letter, and another one he wrote to his grandmother during the same period, show the great maturity of this young monk who later became such a sure spiritual guide. In the letter quoted above the young monk told his grandmother that

4. Quoted by C. Dumont, unpublished.

he thought she would like Guardini's book *The Lord,* and added: "Nicole can read it to you from time to time, just as I used to read Corneille to you in the days when Aunt Rosa preferred to play backgammon rather than to listen to me make myself hoarse by bombastically declaiming *Polyeucte.*"

Dom Anselme's illness

One day in March, 1949, Br. Charles' sister Francine and her fiancé Raymond De Vos, who was also a close friend of Br. Charles, had come to Scourmont for a visit. Dom Anselme spent an hour or so with them, delighting them with his animated and friendly conversation. Just a few days later, to the consternation of everyone, the Abbot suffered a severe stroke, which left him unable to speak and affected his mental and physical capacities. In spite of his disablement he wanted to continue to share in the life of the community, and with assistance did so in every way he could. For the monks the illness of their cherished and venerated abbot was a great trial; he was, indeed, "the head and heart of the community," (4.6.49) as Br. Charles wrote in a letter to his family.

As was the practice in the Order at that time Dom Anselme had been elected abbot for life, but since he could no longer accomplish his duties it was necessary to appoint an Apostolic Administrator. This charge was entrusted to Fr. Guerric Baudet.

Ordination to the Priesthood

Br. Charles was ordained deacon in December, 1949. In his homily at the Eucharist that day the presiding prelate, a White Father of the Society of Missionaries of Africa, remarked that the Trappist life would suit Africans very well. Charles' cousin George, a seminarian in the Société Auxiliaire des Missions preparing for an apostolate in the Middle East observed that the same thing could be said about Arabs and the Trappist life. The next spring on the feast of the Ascension which was May 18 that year, the young deacon was ordained priest by Msgr. Himmer, bishop of Tournai. During the same ceremony George was ordained deacon. A strong lifelong friendship existed between the two cousins: the monk and the missionary.

Not long after Fr. Charles' ordination a providential incident occurred which was to have an influence on his whole monastic life. Dom Jean Leclercq stopped by at Scourmont one day and asked Dom Guerric if one of his monks would be willing to translate Aelred of Rievaulx's *Rule for a Recluse* and *Pastoral Prayer* for *Sources Chrétiennes,* the series of patristic publications recently founded by the eminent Jesuits Henri de Lubac, Claude Mondésert and Jean Daniélou. When this was proposed to Fr. Charles he accepted without hesitation. It was the first time he had done work in depth on Aelred's writings and he undertook it with enthusiasm. Most of his translation of the *Rule for a Recluse* was accomplished at Caldey, because now that he had finished his studies and had been ordained Fr. Charles was soon sent to Caldey Priory to teach philosophy to the young professed monks.

Caldey

The Isle of Caldey is located on Carmarthen Bay, a few miles off the coast of Pembrokeshire. When the weather is good, the trip between its cliffs and the little harbor at Tenby takes more or less a half-hour. It is hard to know with certainty when monks first came to the island, but it is believed that from the sixth century on a small Celtic community lived there. It disappeared in the tenth century when the Danes invaded Caldey, but in the twelfth century monks following the Benedictine way of life were on the island and remained there until the suppression of monasteries by Henry VIII in 1536. Several Welsh saints are traditionally associated with Caldey, notably David, Samson and Gildas. The church on the island is dedicated to Saint David. In 1906 Caldey was bought by monks of the Church of England known as the Reformed Order of Anglican Benedictines. It was these monks who built the present monastery. The Abbot and most of the brothers were received into the Catholic Church in

1913 and the community joined the Benedictine Order not long after. The monks continued to live on the island until 1928, when they moved to Prinknash on the mainland.

At Scourmont, seeing how his community was growing, Dom Anselme Le Bail had been thinking about making a foundation. He looked first toward Spain and then considered India as a possibility. It was only after Pope Pius XI appealed to the Cistercian Order to take over Caldey that his attention turned toward the Island and he accepted this challenge. A group of monks left Scourmont for Wales on December 31, 1928, and arrived at Tenby on January 2, 1929. The weather was so bitterly cold and the wind so strong that the monks had to wait until January 5 to undertake the rough crossing to the island. Dom Anselme formally opened the foundation the next day, the feast of the Epiphany of Our Lord. Five years later the foundation became autonomous and Fr. Aelred Lefèvre, who had been superior since the monks' arrival on the Island, was elected titular prior. In 1942 after Fr. Aelred's untimely death Father Albert Derzelle, prior at Scourmont, was appointed to succeed him as superior. Four years later he was elected titular prior. The following year, in reply to Fr. Albert's desire to open a novitiate, Dom Anselme sent several Scourmont novices to Caldey to bolster the ranks. At that time there had been question also of sending Br. Charles whose presence would have been supportive to Dom Albert, but his health and his studies seemed to indicate that he should stay at Scourmont. At that time, in fact, he was in his third year of theology and had recently received the first two minor orders.

Later on, after his ordination, when Fr. Charles did leave Scourmont for Caldey in December, 1950, he had no idea that he would remain there for ten years. If he had, leaving the monastery and the monks whom he had become so attached to would have made his departure all the more painful. Saying good-bye to Dom Anselme was the hardest. He would always remember how at that moment his beloved abbot, paralyzed and unable to speak, looked at him with tears in his eyes.

Since Fr. Charles had to pass through London on his way to Caldey he took advantage of the stopover to visit Professor C. H. Talbot who was working on an edition of some of Aelred's sermons, later published under the title *Sermones inediti.* When he finally arrived at Caldey, he wrote his family a detailed account of his trip across southern England:

> I have been here at Caldey a week now . . . I was very tired when I arrived after a very unpleasant trip: standing for twelve hours—all night!—in the London-Tenby train. It was three days before Christmas! When I arrived at Tenby, I learned that because of a terrible storm no boats had been able to cross over for three days. Nevertheless, when there finally was a calm for a while they took a chance and I experienced what it is like to be shaken up . . . A monk showed me around the Island. It is marvelous. But the air is very bracing and the change of climate has been very abrupt. Besides that, I am homesick. From my room I have a view of the sea and the Tenby coast which is a constant delight. Below my window, I see cowslips. We can sit outside without a coat. It is a pleasure for me to see Dom Albert again. . . . (Tell Nicole that) in London I noticed several features of women's winter fashions. But I only had a few hours, and I spent half that time bent over old manuscripts in the British Museum. (12.30.50)

It was in reply to a very real need that Fr. Charles had been sent to take in hand the formation of Caldey's young monks. Of the thirty members of the community twelve were in the novitiate. Among the monks present at that time were Fr. John Gran, who later became bishop of Oslo, and Fr. Francis Mahieu, who was biding his time before going to India. Caldey, of course, was very different from Scourmont so that the newcomer had to get adjusted to certain things: for example, the gales which whipped around the island, and the English-speaking but bicultural community. Differences of opinion between the English and the Belgians—particularly about the British custom of having afternoon tea, which literally stirred up a tempest in a teacup—made for an atmosphere quite unlike the one he was used to at Scourmont, where there was such great unity. But he had come to Caldey for a purpose and soon became completely immersed in community life and absorbed with teaching the young monks.

During this whole period Fr. Charles corresponded regularly with Fr. Maur Standaert, who was prior at Scourmont. There was hardly a letter that did not contain a request for one or more volumes from the library of the abbey. When Fr. Charles was perplexed by some theological or philosophical question, he asked Fr. Maur for a lead or reference, or sometimes for a solution. In spite of the fact that he loved the sea and the sea air, his health was not very good. Three months after his arrival, he wrote to his grandmother:

> I am writing to you from "my villa (St Oswald)"—all the rooms in the monastery are occupied! I can study at leisure, typewrite and look at the sea. For the time being, I am on vacation. I like my teaching job and I am beginning to get interested in philosophy, Saint Thomas and my four students: a Polish boy, a former aviator-journalist, and two other Englishmen . . . I was given the job of hunting rabbits, but it would really take a rabbit who is more distracted than the poet I am, and he would have to be right on my path. Rabbits are a big problem for us; they multiply at a prodigious rate. Fr. Prior was thinking about starting a weaving workshop, but now they have turned to raising pigs . . . We do what we can to make ends meet. (3.21.51)

During the next few years Fr. Charles taught courses on metaphysics, ethics, the Sacraments and logic, using Saint Thomas mostly. He was glad he had kept good notes when he took logic at Scourmont! He also taught a History of Philosophy course. After an arid dose of Descartes and Kant he delved into existentialism, which immediately captured his interest. "*Ça mord de plus en plus. . . .*" From that time on the existentialist approach has been one of the main characteristics of Fr. Charles' writings, in which Kierkegaard, Gabriel Marcel and other contemporary philosophers are so frequently referred to and quoted. As he explored these avenues of philosophy, he thought wistfully of Scourmont and asked Fr. Maur: "What's new at the Faculty of Scourmont?" (December, 1951).

While teaching, Fr. Charles was also progressing in his translation of Aelred's *Rule for a Recluse*. In November, 1951, he met again with Professor Talbot in London to discuss the Latin text which would appear with the translation. During this visit he stayed at the Warburg Institute of the University of London, and worked a bit in the Grail library. His letters to Fr. Maur at this time were filled with notations about books, and also questions. "Have you ever run across *disciplina ordinis* in Saint Bernard? *Ordo disciplinae* is a classical expression used by the scholastics, but in the *Vita Ailredi* it says that at the end of his life Aelred spoke to the brothers about nothing but the *disciplina ordinis*. I have ideas for a lot of articles . . . but I will die before that" (1.13.52). When a little later Fr. Maur invited him to give some lectures at Scourmont, he was overjoyed: "I don't hesitate a minute (to say yes). I would like to talk about Aelred and the relationship between action and contemplation . . . or anything else, as long as it is at Scourmont" (8.15.52).

His trips to London were not simply in view of advancing his work on Aelred. He also spent some of his time seeing doctors. "I am in the hands of a Professor of medicine in London. By that I mean that I have become a laboratory specimen on which they try out pills, drugs, injections, etc. Fortunately I am none the worse for it . . . Maybe I will have a holiday next summer and in that case I will bring back all the books from Scourmont's library that you have lent me" (to Fr. Maur, 8.15.52).

Fr. Camille Hontoir, editor of *Collectanea*, the Order's periodical, asked Fr. Charles to review *The Ascent to Truth,* Thomas Merton's recently published book on Saint John of the Cross. This new work of Merton was very different in style and contents from his vastly popular *Seven Storey Mountain*. Fr. Charles' review—his first in *Collectanea,* and a long one—appeared in the last issue of 1952. The author of *The Ascent to Truth* and the reviewer were later to become close friends. Here, let it suffice to say that the review was learned and straightforward, even biting. Fr. Charles pointed out that Merton had more or less gotten lost in a maze of dialectical reasoning and that this would disappoint many of his readers. They would, however, be glad when they would come upon the many deep and spiritually exhilarating passages which were the real Merton, written in his unique style. Briefly, he encouraged Merton to be himself in the future. It is interesting to see that in his *Journal* Merton himself wrote that he thought that this book was "abominable (with) almost no theological insight and no spirit."[5]

The Dijon Congress

The year 1953 marked the eighth centenary of Saint Bernard's death. To highlight this occasion a celebration due mainly to the initiative of Dom Jean Leclercq was held in Dijon in September. For several days lectures were presented on various aspects of the life and spirituality of Saint Bernard. All of these studies were subsequently published in *Saint Bernard théologien*,[6] a prestigious volume which is still consulted and referred to by scholars and monastics. Strange to say, only two Cistercians spoke at this Congress: Fr. Claude Bodard, of Orval, and Fr. Pacificus Delfgaauw, of Tilburg. Several Benedictines, including Dom Jean Leclercq and Dom J-M. Déchanet, presented papers, as did some of the outstanding theologians of the day, such as Fr. Jean Daniélou, SJ, Fr. Yves Congar, OP, and Canon Jean Mouroux. The personalist philosopher Aimé Forest was also among the lecturers. This meeting was scheduled to take place concurrently with the 1953 General Chapter of the Cistercians of the Strict Observance at Cîteaux. In the Acts of the Chapter it was spoken of as being "theological (and) centered on Saint Bernard's thought

5. *A Search for Solitude. The Journals of Thomas Merton*. Volume 3. 1952–1960, edited Lawrence S. Cunningham (San Francisco: Harper San Francisco, 1996) 123. October 5, 1957.

6. *Analecta Cisterciensia*. IX. fasc. 3–4 (Rome: Editiones Cistercienses, 1954).

and teaching."[7] If we read a little further, however, we feel a letdown: "Because the abbots were occupied with the activities of the General Chapter, they could attend only a few of the lectures." What a pity that the abbots did not put aside their discussions on the usages and take time to listen to scholars in the vanguard of the patristic theological movement in the Church talk about the greatest Cistercian theologian of all times. Fr. Charles was in Dijon for this Congress, and if the abbots' attendance at the lectures was sporadic his was not. He wrote to Fr. Maur about this really unique experience:

> Fr. Daniélou spoke very brilliantly about the Greek Fathers, limiting himself to Origen and Gregory of Nyssa. He isn't familiar with your work and thought he was discovering progress in Saint Bernard's thought (on the image) in *On Grace and Free Choice* or the *First Sermon On the Song of Songs*. Fr. (Henri) de Lubac is here and made some extraordinarily clear and precise comments this morning. (After Ivanka's lecture on Scripture) I took the liberty of asking Fr. Claude Bodard if we could call Saint Bernard's theology biblical theology, in the modern sense of the word. This seemed to startle Fr. Daniélou a bit. (September, 1953)

Another scholar present at the Dijon Congress was Fr. Louis Lekai. Fr. Charles had recently published a review of his book *The White Monks* in *Collectanea's Bulletin de spiritualité monastique*. He considered Fr. Lekai to be the best historian on early Cîteaux at that time. Following this memorable meeting Fr. Charles had occasions to correspond with some of the experts he met there, notably Aimé Forest, Fr. de Lubac and Fr. Daniélou, who was going to publish Fr. Charles' article: "Lent, the sacrament of spiritual combat according to saint Bernard" in the magazine *Parole Vivante*. Unfortunately, this periodical was discontinued soon after, so that the article came out only much later, in *Collectanea* (1962-1). That same autumn of 1953, after the Dijon Congress, Fr. Charles had the opportunity to attend another patristic meeting,

7. *Acts*, General Chapter OCSO (Cîteaux: September, 1953) 1.

this time at Oxford. Not long after, the editor of the *Revue diocésaine de Tournai* asked him to contribute an article on Saint Bernard to be published in a 1955 issue on priestly ministry. The title he chose was *Apostolic sense in Saint Bernard.*

Once he was back at Caldey, Fr. Charles began a course on the Sacraments for his six students. Before undertaking the section on the Eucharist he asked Fr. Maur's advice about how to plan his course and received the reply that he should begin with the Eucharist as sacrifice. The young professor wrote back: "You are right. I should have begun with sacrifice. We should always begin with sacrifice, but we always put it off until later" (12.13.55). He and his students also read Hippolytus' *Apostolic Tradition* together. Meanwhile, Dom Albert was thinking about sending the Caldey students to Scourmont the following year for their formation. He had already sent three to the motherhouse and the result had been positive, but he was hesitant because life at Caldey would be more difficult with six young monks away. At Scourmont, in 1954, the community was preparing to make a foundation at Mokoto, in the Kivu region of Zaire.

As usual, Fr. Charles had several irons in the fire. Besides his work with the students he was reading Heidegger and thinking how much he would have liked to have studied with such a master. In the line of his on-going preoccupation with the theme of action-contemplation he was working on a paper on Martha and Mary in Aelred's writings and, in a completely different line, at Fr. Maur's request he was composing a little ditty to be sung to the tune of *Old Black Joe* for the golden jubilee of Brother Eugene, with whom Fr. Charles had worked in the tailor shop at Scourmont.

Professor Aimé Forest's approach to philosophy appealed very much to Fr. Charles. During the meeting on Saint Bernard at Dijon the participants had gone to Fontenay for a special celebration one day. Professor Forest invited Fr. Charles to sit next to him on the bus. On the way the professor told him about the tragedy which had befallen his family during the war. The Forests lived in Laplaud, in Vienne, during the German occupation. In the weeks following D-Day, as allied troops advanced across France there were violent outbursts of Nazi revenge in various places. One of the most frightful occurred at Oradour, near Laplaud. The morning of June 10, Professor Forest went to Limoges, taking three of his children with him. His oldest son, Michel (16), and Dominique, the youngest (6), did not go because they wanted to walk over to Oradour to visit their grandfather that afternoon. When they reached Oradour they found the place swarming with Nazis who were rounding up everyone in sight. They forced the men into a farm building and turned their machine guns on them. The women and children were herded into the church which was then set on fire. Both boys died that day. Oradour came to stand for what was most horrible in World War II.

Aimé Forest's work was especially significant for Cistercians because of its personalist character. The professor must have felt an affinity with Fr. Charles, because shortly after the Congress he wrote him a long letter explaining his approach. Fr. Charles, in turn, wrote to Fr. Maur: "The analysis of these spiritual doctrines (i.e., Cistercian), or rather, of spiritual experience, appears to him to be the foundation of the metaphysical truths which are accessible to us," and he added: "What riches we can draw from our authors!" (11.11.54). The monk and the philosopher continued to correspond.

During Advent, 1954, Dom Christopher Butler of Downside Abbey preached the annual retreat at Caldey. Not only did he have vast knowledge of monastic spirituality but he was also a poet, so that Fr. Charles was doubly won over by him. In fact, he said that he found this retreat to be a pure marvel. And as the year drew to an end he was finalizing his article on "The balanced life of the monk according to Blessed Aelred of Rievaulx," the ripened fruit of his reflection on Martha and Mary—action and contemplation.

If we judge by all this activity, we might be led to think that Fr. Charles' health had improved. The truth is that his ailments gave him little respite, and after the retreat with Dom Butler he had to be hospitalized. As he left the monastery he picked up a book at random, which as it happened was a volume of Saint

Cyprian's works. During the time he was at Saint Winifred's Hospital in Cardiff, in the care of Irish nursing sisters, he spent many hours absorbed in this book with the result that he was inspired to write an article on *lectio divina*. He wrote to Fr. Maur that he was disintoxicated from metaphysical spirituality. Cyprian's use of the term *disciplina* interested him especially. "A discipline for life, a clear and vigorous type of Christianity; the essential thing that Forest talks about constantly. It is there that it is found: in faith and constancy in Christ" (12.16.54).

As for his medical report, which apparently interested him less than Cyprian did, the X-rays did not reveal anything requiring an operation. He was told, in fact, that he was in excellent health! And yet, his malaise did not go away.

The Interpreter

The next year brought new experiences. Dom Gabriel Sortais, the Abbot General, asked Fr. Charles to accompany him and his secretary, Fr. Clement de Bourmont, as interpreter during his regular visitations in the monasteries of the British Isles. It was an excellent opportunity for Fr. Charles to enlarge his knowledge of the Order and to make new contacts and friendships. Simply being in the company of Dom Gabriel during the visitations was an education in itself. During the course of the next few years two successive abbots of Melleray asked him to serve as interpreter during regular visitations at Mount Melleray: first Dom Louis de Gonzague Le Pennuen, and then Dom Columban Bissey.

Sources Chrétiennes

Several months after Fr. Charles' tour of the monasteries of the Isles with Dom Gabriel he received a long letter from Fr. Placide Deseille, a monk of Bellefontaine. On Dom Gabriel's suggestion, Fr. Placide asked Fr. Charles to collaborate with him in working something out concerning publication of Cistercian texts in *Sources Chrétiennes*. This interested Fr. Charles, of course, because the text of Aelred he was translating was supposed to be for this series. Fr. Placide had already been in contact with Fr. Jean Daniélou who, with Frs. Henri de Lubac and Claude Mondésert, formed the board of directors. For several reasons unanimity had not been reached about adding medieval texts to the patristic collection: there were more patristic translations ready and waiting for publication than could be published, the funds available were limited and the scholarly character of *Sources Chrétiennes* meant that the volumes would be necessarily high-priced. After discussion, it was decided that the two volumes of Aelred: *Jesus at the Age of Twelve* and *Rule for a Recluse,* being prepared by Dom Anselme Hoste and Fr. Charles respectively, would definitely be published, but another solution would have to be found for other Cistercian texts. There were, in fact, about twenty monks and nuns in various monasteries who were already working on translations.

The Cistercians proposed an alternate solution: a collection of medieval spiritual texts parallel to *Sources Chrétiennes,* under the auspices of the Order. Fr. Charles described this project in a letter to Fr. de Lubac who passed the information on to Fr. Mondésert. This was Fr. Charles' first occasion to write to Fr. de Lubac, but from then on they corresponded for many years. In October, 1956, Fr. Placide met with Fr. Mondésert, Dom Déchanet and the directors of Les Editions du Cerf. Together they worked out a plan for a series within *Sources Chrétiennes* to be entitled: *Textes monastiques d'Occident,* for both Cistercian and other medieval monastic texts. As it happened, Dom Gabriel Sortais was in Paris at that time, so he too was able to discuss the project with Fr. Mondésert and Dom Déchanet and was very pleased with it. The first volume in this series came out in 1958: Dom Anselme Hoste's edition of Aelred of Rievaulx's *Jesus at the Age of Twelve*. These intricate negotiations with Le Cerf and the directors of *Sources Chrétiennes* show that serious efforts to make French translations of Cistercian texts available to monks and nuns of the Order date from before Vatican II.

Dom Eugene Boylan

The 1950s were important years for both Caldey and Scourmont. The work involved in developing the community on the Island had taken such a toll on Dom Albert's health that he was obliged to resign, but thanks to his influence and accomplishments Caldey now had hope for the future. Dom Albert returned to Scourmont toward the end of 1955. It was not easy for Fr. Charles to see him go. The new superior, Dom Eugene Boylan, an Irishman with a strong and colorful personality, is probably best known for his book on mental prayer, but he was also a highly-qualified scientist. After earning a Ph.D. from the University of Vienna and teaching physics at the University of Dublin, Dom Eugene entered Roscrea and was later sent to Tarrawarra, Roscrea's foundation in Australia. When he became superior at Caldey his mother, who was directress of the Summer School of Gregorian chant at the University of Dublin, would sometimes come to visit him. On these occasions this imposing monk was on edge that after listening to the community chant the Divine Office she would tell him: "It's all wrong, my boy." Fr. Charles wrote Fr. Maur about his first conversation with Dom Eugene: "He started talking to me right away about matter and form (*realiter vel rationaliter distinctae*), and just as I was about to reply I seemed to hear you saying (10 years ago . . .) 'Most Thomist philosophers today speak of a logical distinction.' I was saved!!!" (2.15.55).

Dom Eugene appointed Fr. Charles master of students; and although he confided to his former mentor that "the function is as inept as the title," (3.5.55) he nevertheless plunged into ethics in Saint Thomas. To help him prepare his course, he asked for Scourmont's copy of Aristotle's *Nicomachean Ethics,* and at the same time for the two-volume work of Roger Troisfontaine, SJ, on Gabriel Marcel: *De l'existence à l'être.* Marcel's type of existentialism interested him more and more. A little later he was overjoyed when he received an invitation to give the homily at Scourmont on the feast of Saint Bernard. "I asked Dom Eugene for permission to come . . . That way, I think he will be freer to ask me to come back if he really wants me (at Caldey)" (8.8.55). On his way to Scourmont he stopped at Steenbrugge to see Dom Anselme Hoste, who had completed his critical edition and translation of Aelred's *Jesus at the Age of Twelve*.

Death of Dom Anselme Le Bail

On September 25, 1956, Dom Anselme Le Bail died after his long illness. The chronicle in *Collectanea* paid him this sober tribute:

> Everyone knows what he did during his long years as abbot, twice troubled by war, to promote studies especially on the history, spirituality and liturgy of the Order, and at the same time to organize a library suitable for this work . . . Although Dom Anselme was paralyzed for almost eight years, unable to speak and obliged to live in the infirmary, he loved to be with the community whenever he could. A brother took him to church in his wheelchair on Feast Days. We might find him in the brewery or at the farm; and when work in the fields was heaviest and most urgent we would see him in the fields farthest from the monastery. We saw him; he was there, always smiling, always interested in everything and in everyone. Always an abbot, always a father.[8]

A short notice on Dom Anselme's role in founding *Collectanea* was published in the same issue as the above chronicle. The editor, Fr. Camille Hontoir, summarized in a few lines Dom Anselme's monastic vision which marked the monks of his community so indelibly and which today is still a sure guide for anyone who takes the trouble to explore it:

> (As novice master) he studied and taught the spirituality of the Order with the keenest and most perspicacious zeal. Word by word he analyzed the works of Cistercian authors

8. "Chroniques de nos Abbayes. Scourmont," *Collectanea Cisterciensia* 19 (1957). Supplement to Fascicule 2: 22.

> of the first centuries of the Order as perhaps no one else had ever done before; he brought out all the doctrine hidden in them. Nothing escaped him in his research. Also, and especially, he coordinated his findings, giving each item its proper value. Together, these form a whole, a veritable sum of teaching material. Father Abbot wrote and gave his courses in French, avoiding dry terminology. He was careful to underline what was essential, but with the ease and flowing style which only those who possess a broad general culture and real humanism have at their command.[9]

If this digression on Dom Anselme's teaching at Scourmont has been inserted here, it is to show the foundation on which Fr. Charles Dumont's monastic teaching is based. He learned his method from Dom Anselme, a method more pertinent for the study of Cistercian spirituality than any which can be acquired in a university. This does not mean that Fr. Charles simply copied Dom Anselme. Just as Aelred of Rievaulx's writings were strongly influenced by Saint Bernard but are at the same time original and personalized, so Fr. Charles' teaching, based on Dom Anselme's, is original and personalized, especially because of his interest in philosophy and literature, and by the fact that he is a poet.

Election of Guerric Baudet

On November 30 Dom Guerric Baudet, Apostolic Administrator of Scourmont during the years of Dom Anselme's illness, was elected abbot. Fr. Charles attended the abbatial blessing on December 8, then returned to Caldey. It was on one of these trips to the island that an incident occurred which in later years became one of his favorite stories. A friend had driven Fr. Charles and another young monk to the train station at Hirson, where they were to catch the Rome-Calais express scheduled to come through toward the end of the morning. When they got to the station the three men continued their conversation while waiting. There was a train on one of the tracks, but nothing was going on and there

9. "Dom Anselme LeBail et les *Collectanea*." *Collectanea* 19 (1957) 82–83.

was no one around, so they didn't give it a second thought. Besides, the train from Rome was practically always late, often very late. Finally the train in the station slowly started to pull out and Father Charles thought it might be a good idea to check on when the Calais train was expected. The agent told him that it had just left. Horrified, the three men raced to the car and drove as fast as they could to the next station. When they arrived the train was just about to leave, so once again the two travelers had to run. The other monk ran faster than Fr. Charles and got on the second-last car, whereas Father Charles jumped onto the platform of the last car and flopped down in a compartment, completely out of breath. When his emotions calmed down he suddenly realized that the train was not moving. He looked around and saw that he was the only one in the car. It had been uncoupled! Uncoupling the last cars was ordinary procedure as passengers got off at different stations on long hauls such as from Rome to Calais.

Fr. Charles' translation of Thomas Merton's article on "Monastic Formation according to Adam of Perseigne" appeared in French in *Collectanea* 1957-1, followed in the 1957-2 issue by the results of his painstaking research on manuscripts of Aelred's *Sermons On the Burdens of Isaiah*. Once back on the island, he resumed his philosophy courses. He was increasingly captivated by the works of Cardinal Newman, from which he drew material for his classes on epistemology and apologetics. In a letter to Fr. Maur at Easter he quoted this beautiful phrase from Newman's Sermon 8 on the Resurrection: "We do feel joy, we feel more joy than we know we do. We see more of the next world than we know we see." He was also reading the excellent work on Newman by J.-F. Walgrave, a Dominican of Louvain.

By the end of 1957, with the help of a small commission for studies, the student master had been able to organize a weekly program of ten hours of class for theology students and seven hours for those in philosophy. This was quite an achievement in a community of approximately forty monks who had a lot of manual work to do. He had also finished his Introduction to *The Rule for a Recluse*.

In December, Fr. Maur's mother died. Fr. Charles had known Madame Standaert, and wrote to Fr. Maur:

> Today I received the notice of your mother's death. What can I say to you? In English they say *sympathy* instead of *condolence,* and that is closer to *compassio*. I remember your mother and I could see that she had great affection for you. Perhaps those who have been deprived of maternal affection too soon notice such things more than others do, with a bit of envy . . . My heartfelt prayer for the repose of her soul.
>
> Yesterday I gave the sermon for the Epiphany, and I spoke almost exclusively about the beatific vision. I remember that when my father died my mind was completely absorbed by the mystery of the afterlife, as if I was trying to follow him and know what kind of life he was living after he left us . . . . (1.7.58)

In 1958 and 1959 Fr. Charles was teaching five or six hours of philosophy classes each week, and had become particularly interested in theodicy. In addition to teaching, he was busy in the tailor shop and also did some outside work when his health would permit it. Not long after Dom Guerric's blessing as abbot, Fr. Charles had written to him: "My classes tire me quite a lot, and last week I wasn't well. And yet, I have put aside everything else to devote myself exclusively to my courses." He added:

> I feel less and less capable of definitions. Instead of defining, limiting, it seems to me that we should unite, include (*comprendre*), show the relationships between all things, find the single principle; but it escapes us as soon as we get a glimpse of it, and this impossibility to embrace the whole, and to lose in finesse what we gain in depth leaves me with a feeling of weariness. (2.21.57)

Fr. Maur suggested that he write a biography of Dom Anselme Le Bail, but Fr. Charles replied that what he would really like to do was to go back over Dom Anselme's works on the Cistercian authors. Meanwhile, he had been asked to present a paper explaining the new series of *Textes Monastiques d'Occident* of Cerf Editions at a Patristic Conference at Magdalen College, Oxford. After this meeting, which took place in September, 1959, Fr. Charles headed home to Scourmont. On the ferry crossing the Channel he met some young clergymen and they found each other's company very enjoyable. Several weeks after he had returned to Belgium he received a clipping from the chronicle: *The Cowley Evangelist*, containing the following few lines contributed by one of those young clerics:

> *S. André-Saint-Gérard-Chevetogne.* Abbaye de S. André-lez-Bruges, 30 Sept. 1959. I met Brother Anselm at Victoria for the 10 a.m. train yesterday. We had a most *delightful* journey here, in every way. The crossing (3 ½ hours) was quite perfect—lovely sunshine, smooth sea, fresh breeze—what more could one wish? To complete our enjoyment a very nice Belgian priest looking like an English clergyman introduced himself to us. He was returning from the Patristic Conference in Oxford and proved to be Père Charles Dumont, OCR, of the Trappist monastery of Scourmont near Chimay. One could not have a more entirely delightful companion, with a great sense of humour. We all had lunch together and did our best to put the affairs of the world and the Church to rights before we landed.[10]

In April, 1961, Fr. Charles was again asked to be interpreter during several regular visitations in Ireland. It was a taxing job at Mount Melleray because there were one hundred and twenty-five religious to see the visitor. At Roscrea he found Dom Eugene Boylan, who had returned to the monastery of his profession when Dom Samson (James) Wicksteed became Prior at Caldey in 1959. Dom Eugene appeared to be in excellent form and it was obvious that his presence had a very positive effect on the

10. *The Cowley Evangelist* is the journal of the English Congregation of the Society of Saint John the Evangelist. The clipping was from the November, 1959, issue.

community. When Roscrea's aged Abbot Camillus resigned the next year the monks elected Dom Eugene to succeed him. All in all, Fr. Charles was very impressed by the monastic life he saw at Roscrea. There was a certain charm about the place, enhanced by beautiful weather during his whole stay. Quite innocently one evening at table he mentioned that Belgian children learn in geography class that it rains every other day in Ireland. Indignant, Dom Camillus replied that this was a lie spread by the English!

When Fr. Charles returned to Caldey in May he found a stack of copies of Aelred's *La Vie d'une Recluse et la Prière Pastorale* which had just come off the press. Before long he began to receive encouraging notes about his work from scholars including Dom Hoste, Professor Talbot, Aelred Squire and Amédée Hallier, but he remarked with modesty that "they had not yet had time really to read the book." Fr. Maur congratulated him with all the warmth that an experienced monk feels toward a younger one who has grown his wings. Still, he did point out some minute errors in the notes which had escaped the editor's scrutiny. This dismayed Fr. Charles a bit, even though Fr. Maur—borrowing an expression used by a fellow monk—assured him that to find them had been like hunting for fleas in a lion's mane. For Fr. Charles' Father Abbot that was not so. Opening the first copy which arrived at Scourmont, he immediately saw what he considered to be quite a big flea: a word which had an extra letter! Fortunately, Father Charles was used to Dom Guerric's sense of humor.

Three monks were ordained at Caldey in June, 1961. It must have given their mentor satisfaction to see that after years of hard work, his and theirs, they had arrived at this important moment in their Christian and monastic life. He reflected on his own spiritual journey: "This year I will be in the monastic life twenty years. Already twenty years since Dom Anselme launched *La Blanche Nef* on the waves of his imagination, and here I am, washed ashore on this Island" (6.29.61).

In 1962, Fr. Charles left Caldey definitively to return to Scourmont. In the future he would visit the island from time to time, but henceforth Scourmont was his home base. The monk who returned was the same as the one who had departed in 1950, yet very different. He had left the dynamic life at Scourmont as a newly-ordained priest to assume responsibilities in a struggling, still fairly new community. His work at Caldey, first with Dom Albert, then with Dom Eugene, for the intellectual and spiritual formation of the student monks and at the same time his personal work on Saint Aelred and Saint Bernard, in spite of frequent illness, had required a tremendous output of energy, application and perseverance. When he returned to Scourmont he had become a recognized scholar and an experienced spiritual guide and teacher. He had published eleven articles—chiefly on Saint Bernard and Saint Aelred—in both periodicals and collective works, in addition to the *Rule for a Recluse* and a volume of selected texts of Aelred for the Soleil Levant series. A new chapter of his life was about to open. Not long after his return he was asked to preach a retreat at Scourmont to a group of priests. Then in January, 1963, Dom Guerric appointed him resident chaplain of the nuns of Notre-Dame de la Paix, at Chimay, and also editor and administrator of *Collectanea*.

3

YEARS OF CHANGE, BEFORE AND AFTER VATICAN II

Borne by the Spirit of his vocation, (the monk) becomes a link in the chain of Tradition, receiving life from the texts themselves, and in whatever way it may please God transmitting it to others.

C. D.

The New Editor of Collectanea

Although Scourmont is only a few miles from Chimay, when Fr. Charles became chaplain of the nuns of Notre-Dame de la Paix Abbey he resided there. He succeeded as chaplain Dom Godefroid Bélorgey who after being Abbot of Cîteaux had returned to Scourmont, his original monastery. Once Fr. Charles was settled in the stone house on a narrow street at the edge of the monastery property in the tranquil principality of Chimay, he organized his work as editor and also administrator of *Collectanea*. His time was divided between selecting and editing articles, keeping the books and contacts with the printer. In addition, there were sermons and conferences to prepare for the nuns, and of course confessions.

Since the approval of *Collectanea* by the 1933 General Chapter it had always been more or less an official organ of the Order. Abbot General Herman Joseph Smets had been the first editor, even though he delegated full responsibility for the magazine to Scourmont's Fr. Camille Hontoir, who managed it for twenty years. Then from 1955 until 1959 the Definitor Dom André Fracheboud was in charge of *Collectanea,* and from 1959 until 1962 Dom André Louf. It was after Dom André's election as abbot of Mont-des-Cats that Fr. Charles was appointed editor of the magazine, which was still under the authority of the Generalate in Rome.

A part of Fr. Charles' assignment consisted in editing the *Bulletin de spiritualité monastique*. This kept him in contact with many outstanding authors, and also with just about everything that was being written on monastic subjects. A number of Cistercian monks and nuns were already writing reviews for the *Bulletin.* Others joined their ranks during the next few years. The editor himself contributed an increasing number of reviews, especially of books and articles on the Cistercian Fathers and contemporary monasticism. Myriad are the reviews which during the following years were signed simply "C.D."

As it was, the first issue edited by Fr. Charles came out early in 1963, directly following the opening of the Second Vatican Council. Until that time *Collectanea* had been a medium for quality articles on the theology and spirituality of the Cistercian Fathers, as well as on Cistercian history and architecture. Now it was going to navigate in uncharted waters, unsheltered from the winds which were blowing in the Church during and after the Council. Throughout this whole difficult period, critical for Cistercians as well as for all religious institutes, in his own quiet self-effacing way Charles Dumont was at the helm of *Collectanea* as a means of communication for the Order. With a sureness that was the fruit of his formation under Dom Anselme Le Bail, he instinctively kept the contents of the review within constructive channels, avoiding the reefs of polemics and contestation but observing and listening to everything coming from all corners of the monastic world. Sr. Lorraine Caza, CND, in her article for *Collectanea's* fiftieth anniversary in 1988, observed: "The great turning point in the review which I saw in Tomes 24–27 must have coincided with the beginning of their years as editors (i.e., Fr. Charles and his assistant, Brother Gabriel Ghislain). I would like to call them *architects of the second wind (souffle).*"[1]

Fr. Charles' first issue in 1963 began with a rather long editorial on tradition, in which he set forth the policies which *Collectanea* was going to follow. While recognizing the value of the avalanche of erudite historical and critical studies which were beginning to appear in various books and periodicals, he stressed the need to keep them in balance with interiority and personal experience. He also showed that a return to the sources was not something new but actually ancient, bound to the very nature of the Church:

> Tradition does not belong only to the past. It is not identified with a particular moment in history . . . but with the living source from which, at this very moment today, our Christian experience flows forth . . . Historical research, indispensable as it may be, is only a preparatory step for understanding Tradition, because works of erudition do not coincide infallibly with its soul. The Spirit is ever re-creating and guiding the Church . . . Too little has been done in the area of rethinking the monastic ideal in a biblical perspective, which was always the primary concern of the ancient monks . . . The quantity of material produced by scientific research, precious as it may be, risks blocking the path which alone can give our hearts the true key to Tradition. . . . In order to judge tradition, we must participate in it . . . Only a monk who is truly borne by the Spirit of his vocation can assimilate the tradition in a living way and give it this providential significance; in his own life, first of all, and sometimes by his words and writings . . . Reading the texts, ruminating them in his heart, the monk becomes a link in the chain of Tradition, by receiving life from the texts themselves, and in whatever way it may please God, transmitting it to others . . . The Spirit has never been lacking. But to recognize the voice of the Spirit in the texts the

1. Sr. Lorraine Caza, CND, "Mon passionnant Chantier cistercien," *Collectanea* 50 (1988) 24.

> monk must first learn how to listen to him in his life, and first of all in his own personal experience. He must have reached the point where he recognizes this Tradition in every word of his abbot or seniors, in every act of obedience and renunciation, in every grace of prayer with which the Lord has adorned the hearts of his brothers.[2]

Fr. Charles soon realized that in order to keep astride of the times *Collectanea* would have to take on a new character and look. Contributors needed to be able to express their ideas freely, without official supervision. Thomas Merton was also very aware of the magazine's need for change, and thought that it might be best to solicit more articles from non-Cistercian writers, at least for a while.[3] In his short editorial in the next to last issue of 1964, Fr. Charles wrote:

> While the monastic life is seeking necessary adaptations in order to remain faithful to its vocation, it would be astonishing to see a monastic periodical take no interest in the problems concerning the monastic life to which other general interest publications are giving considerable attention. Should *Collectanea* put aside these questions which lead to discussion or divergence of opinions? . . . Without becoming an open forum, our magazine should remain receptive to articles which include constructive criticism and suggestions relative to the monastic life as we are trying to live it today, following the example of our forebears. This presupposes a certain amount of liberty to express opinions for which the Order does not normally assume the responsibility.[4]

He added that even Dom Herman Joseph Smets, when he first introduced *Collectanea,* had said that the review could not assume responsibility for the views of the authors whose articles it published. Fr. Charles' words were heeded, and the 1964/4

2. C. Dumont, "Écouter la Tradition," *Collectanea* 25 (1963) 3–6 passim.

3. See Thomas Merton, Letter to Dom Jean Leclercq, August 28, 1964. In *The School of Charity. Letters on Religious Renewal and Spiritual Direction,* ed. Br. Patrick Hart, ocso (New York: Farrar, Straus, Giroux, 1990) 231.

4. C. Dumont, Editorial. *Collectanea* 26 (1964/3), introductory pages.

issue was the last to bear the words: *Direction—Le Définitoire de l'Ordre Cist. S.O.* Beginning with the first issue of 1965 the magazine had a new Board of Directors composed of two abbots, two monks chosen for their competence, and one Definitor.

This issue, which could be called a key issue, contained articles by Dom André Louf and Thomas Merton on the nature and function of a monastic review, two articles on tradition and aggiornamento and, lastly, two articles on the important subject of studies for monks: one by Fr. Basil Morison (Father Master of Students at Monte Cistello, the Order's Generalate in Rome) and the other by Fr. Placide Deseille. With his teaching experience Fr. Charles understood the great importance of formation in this post-Vatican II time of change. Because these articles proposed what we might call guidelines not only for superiors and monastics involved in formation but for anyone living the monastic life in a monastery, two passages from this issue are quoted here at length. The first is by Thomas Merton who, when he submitted his article, had written to the editor that he was looking forward to seeing *Collectanea* with its new look.

> Without neglecting the authority and certitude of science, the magazine must be dedicated above all to the living and life-giving wisdom which "edifies" in so far as it is born of love for monastic truth. *Caritas aedificat*. This truth is experienced and shared in the tradition handed down by the Fathers. A monastic review's ambition should be no less than to help the monk enter into the heritage of living and experiential wisdom which has come down to him from his Fathers . . . In a time of change like ours, a review has a very important duty of providing necessary materials for study which will enable us to arrive at new solutions that are in harmony with our ancient tradition. . . . The review should be at the heart of a living "conference," a *collatio,* in which the thoughts, research, readings, aspirations, problems and experience of the whole *ordo monasticus* are "brought together" in focus.[5]

5. Thomas Merton, "The Function of a Monastic Review," *Collectanea* 27 (1965) 11–13.

The second text began with a question which the author, Fr. Basil Morison, had asked his professor of Dogma at the Angelicum when he was a student: "How should theology be taught?" The professor replied: "No two Religious Orders can study theology in the same way . . . It all depends on why you want theology." From there, Fr. Basil expounded why he believed Cistercians should study theology:

> Studies should prepare the young monk for his life as a member of a contemplative order, and make it possible for him to live it better because he will have a deeper understanding of what it is all about . . . Philosophy means wondering about the world and all that we know as reality, then thinking hard so as to penetrate more deeply into that reality—above all the two greatest realities, God and ourselves . . . Theology could be described in much the same terms, and inevitably, since there is always a compenetration of philosophy and theology, but theology is more realistic still, considering as it does the full spiritual reality, that is, not only the fact that we exist and that God exists, but that he is intensely interested in every individual and wants, so to speak, to get into contact with him and invite him to the incredible privilege of sharing in his own life . . . Monastic life means, as far as I can see, setting up a state of affairs where the only purpose in life is to enter as fully as possible into this Story of Salvation.[6]

Father Basil stressed that students "must be trained to read accurately, to summarize objectively, to find the relevant literature on a given topic for themselves, to judge its value, and finally—a much neglected point—to express what they think about it all."[7] He also stressed that a little goes a long way in the monastic life.

Father Charles must have been very glad to have such articles to publish. The objective principles firmly spelled out by highly-qualified monks corresponded perfectly to his own convictions.

6. Basil Morison, OCSO, "Studies for Monks," *Collectanea* 27 (1965) passim, 60–61.

7. Ibid., 63.

The second issue in 1965 included articles by Dom Adelbert de Vogüé and Dom Jean Leclercq on an equally urgent topic: monastic life and contemplative life. Dom Leclercq, a regular contributor to *Collectanea,* could always be counted on not only for his phenomenal erudition but also for his stimulating remarks and questions.

The next year, when Fr. Patrick Catry of Mont-des-Cats accepted to edit the *Bulletin* Fr. Charles felt considerably relieved, because on recommendation of his doctor he was leaving for Switzerland for several weeks of rest at Soldanelle, Château d'Oex. At the end of his stay there his health had not improved, so that when he returned to Belgium he went to stay for a while with his sister Nicole at Wenduine on the coast. There he had ample leisure to contemplate the sea which he loved so much. The austere January seascape prompted him to write:

> Waves beginning ever anew, without hope,
> You console so well our vain human efforts;
> You die, you are born, marvelous patience,
> Lost dreams, waves slipping through our fingers.
>
> Soft rumble on the threshold of vast silence,
> Your long verses quieted to the rhythm of a soothing
> lullaby,
> Murmured tenderly like a confidence,
> Brought to my mind a sister's gentleness.[8]

In a letter to Dom Guerric for his birthday in early August, Fr. Charles confided that he had been obliged to ask the members of the *Collectanea* Board of Directors to postpone their meeting until a week later because he was not well enough to travel or to attend a meeting. His doctor was baffled by the way he was wasting away and sent him to see a specialist at Saint Raphael's Clinic, the Flemish-language hospital associated with Louvain University. There his case was finally diagnosed as Crohn's disease, which he learned was a rather rare intestinal disorder. He

8. *"Les Vagues,"* in *Poèmes et Prières,* 17.

was assured that he would never have to undergo an operation for it, and that no one ever died of this illness.

Before the year was out he was able to give a series of lectures on *lectio divina* to the Benedictine nuns at Louvain. He was also chosen to be an expert—consultant for the post-Vatican II Constitutions Commission set up by the 1967 General Chapter of the Order.

To mark the eighth centenary of the death of Saint Aelred of Rievaulx, the first issue of *Collectanea* in 1967 was devoted chiefly to articles on Aelred's works and monastic teaching. Although Fr. Charles himself did not contribute an article for this issue, in place of an editorial he inserted a passage from *The Mirror of Charity* (III.36) which clearly expressed what might be called a message from Aelred to the Order at that time of renewal and experimentation with observances. In this passage on what the Abbot of Rievaulx called the *voluntary order* (*ordo volontarius*), he emphasized that it is by charity that we approach God and become conformed to Him. Charity is the monk's ultimate goal. He strives toward it in the type of life to which he has willingly committed himself by his profession. As to dispensations from observances in the monastic life, Aelred was careful to add that even though the abbot may modify some practices according to the needs and aptitudes of individual monks, he should not omit established practices or change the times fixed for them. Otherwise, he said, there would not be dispensation but disintegration. During the years to come Fr. Charles frequently commented on this passage, because it provides lasting and useful guidelines.

Toward the beginning of March Fr. Charles was obliged to return to Soldanelle for another month's rest. On his way back to Chimay he made a detour to attend an international meeting on Canon Law at Gavirate, near Genoa. His return to Scourmont did not mean that his illness was cured. He did not know it—fortunately for him—but his debilitating and exhausting illness was to be his constant companion for years to come. In spite of periods of absence from Chimay, Fr. Charles' work on *Collectanea* continued uninterruptedly. He prefaced the next issue of the review, centered on Buddhist and Hindu monks, with an editorial on *The monastic phenomenon* from which the following lines are taken:

> Humanity is becoming more and more aware of its unity. This fact, which the Constitution *Lumen Gentium* points out in its very first paragraph, is increasing the Church's awareness of its ecumenical responsibility. Consequently, it is taking an interest in non-Christian religions to encourage them by its sympathy and esteem in a world that has become indifferent to religious values. Monks have their share of responsibility for this reconciliation.[9]

One monk who made a contribution to this issue was his former confrere at Scourmont, Fr. Francis Mahieu, who by that time had founded Kurisumala ashram in Kerala, India. To stimulate the interest of monastic communities in non-Christian religions the editor of *Collectanea* asked Thomas Merton to handle the section of the *Bulletin* dealing particularly with Buddhism and Zen.

Thomas Merton

Fr. Charles was obliged to return to Soldanelle toward the end of 1967. It was there that he received a letter from Dom Columban, Abbot of Melleray, asking him to accompany him as translator during the regular visitation he was going to make at Our Lady of Gethsemani Abbey, Melleray's daughter-house in the United States. Dom James Fox had given his resignation and the community was going to elect a new abbot in January. Poor health or not, Fr. Charles did not intend to miss this chance of going to America. His reply to Dom Columban was affirmative. A visit to Gethsemani meant an opportunity not only to see what monastic life was like in the United States, but finally to meet Thomas Merton, this "friend above all others," as he called him. The two monks had many things in common: the early years of

9. C. Dumont, "Le phénomène monastique," *Collectanea* 29 (1967) 129.

each were lived in French culture, each had lost his mother at an early age, both were poets, both suffered from an almost similar chronic illness, both had the ideal of a more contemplative life in the Order. Fr. Charles' first indirect contact with Merton dated from his biting critique of *The Ascent to Truth* in the *Bulletin*[10] which "met with Merton's humble agreement,"[11] but it was around the time of the publication of *The Sign of Jonas* that the two monks began to exchange letters regularly. *The Sign of Jonas* was different from the monastic literary style of that period, so different that three censors had been asked to evaluate it whereas ordinarily there were only two. One of these censors, a learned and saintly monk, had hesitated to approve it because of certain passages which did not concern the spiritual life specifically, especially those where Merton mentioned details of daily life in community. Yet it was precisely the realistic, personalized way he described life in a monastic community that made this book so attractive. The Epilogue: *Fire Watch. July 4, 1952,* became a classic. And when Merton wrote about perspiration trickling down his neck during adoration of the Blessed Sacrament the reader understood that piety has its price. In his first extant letter to Fr. Charles, dated September 2, 1953, Merton wrote:

> Thank you for your kind words about *Jonas*. It is a problematical book, in the Order. Many have not liked it. I did not expect them to. Dom Leclercq thinks it will not be too well liked in Europe either. The Dutch publishers are afraid to bring out a translation. The book, they say, is not phlegmatic enough for Holland. In that case I shall have to resign myself to the loss of Holland, as I am not at all phlegmatic.[12]

Merton then added: "Where did the legend arise that I would be going to Dijon? My journeys are all into the woods here." He was referring to the Congress on the occasion of the

10. See Chapter 2 of this book, pp. 21–22.

11. C. Dumont, "The Cistercian Beneath the Surface," *Cistercian Studies* 13 (1978) 331.

12. Ibid., (quoting Thomas Merton, letter of September 2, 1953) 325.

eighth centenary of Saint Bernard's death, mentioned in Chapter 2 of this book.[13] Before closing this letter he asked Fr. Charles to pray for him and his scholastics, who had recently given some very good conferences on Saint Bernard. Merton was still a fairly young monk himself, and his university training had left him with a natural enthusiasm for formation.

For some time already Fr. Charles had been thinking about how advantageous it would be to have an English-language periodical parallel to *Collectanea*. The Order was growing in English-speaking countries and Cistercian monks and nuns needed more than an occasional translated article in *Collectanea.* As early as the summer of 1956 (though at that time he had no real connection with *Collectanea*) Fr. Charles had sounded Merton out a bit timidly on this subject. His answer was:

> As for an American Cistercian magazine, I think the hopes are very poor: it would probably turn into a rather cheap sheet full of news bulletins to seduce rich benefactors. I regret that I can offer no better hope for the time being. Perhaps in ten years from now the outlook might be better. England, I should think, would be a better prospect.[14]

Correspondence between the two monks continued regularly, especially after Fr. Charles became editor of *Collectanea* and Merton became a steady contributor to the *Bulletin*. In 1964, Fr. Charles invited Merton to become a member of the board of editors of *Collectanea.* Merton cautiously replied that it would be better to take that matter up with his abbot or with the Abbot General. In his next letter, he explained more clearly what he was really thinking: "Confidentially, my Abbot is going to allow me to move a little more in the direction of solitude and I think it would be better if I did not have any such commitments. So for my own part I am quite reluctant to accept. If of course my Superiors want me to take the job, that is another matter."[15]

13. See Chapter 2, pp. 22–23.

14. "The Cistercian . . . ," (Letter of August 16, 1956) 325–326.

15. Ibid. (Letter of December 4, 1964) 327.

Merton's article on *The Function of a Monastic Review* appeared in the first issue of *Collectanea* in 1965.[16] Around that time the members of the board of editors of the magazine were planning a meeting at which they would study, among other things, the question of an English-language Cistercian magazine. Quite innocently the editor invited his friend Merton, whose presence would certainly have been useful at this meeting. Alas, this letter had unexpected repercussions. First of all there was Merton's reply that he would like to be able to help, but that it was not for him to take the initiative:

> I ought to wait in silence for an expression of God's will—a clear expression—on which my superiors will agree. I suppose that it is my superiors themselves who will let me know what I should do. I wait, before God, without any personal preference, ready to do what he asks me. I leave to you to do what you feel is best. You will no doubt tell me how I should go about this, but I don't think I can ask for something that will certainly be refused . . . I think it is very important to get *Cistercian Studies* started, to be really able to make something out of it, and it is not enough to keep putting it off as has been done. In the present state of the Order, a good magazine is very necessary, because there is a lot of confusion in people's minds, at least in America. Formation is lacking.[17]

Several weeks later Fr. Charles received a letter from Abbot General Dom Ignace Gillet, who had learned from Fr. André Fracheboud about Merton's invitation. He advised Fr. Charles not to try to persuade Merton to come to Chimay unless he knew that Dom James agreed. Dom Ignace's letter was straightforward and respectful, but the fact that the whole matter had taken on dramatic dimensions shows how dangerous indirectly learned information can be, especially since communication in two different

16. See Chapter 3, page 40, with note 5.

17. "Lettres au rédacteur du *Collectanea*," Letter dated June 18, 1965, written in French. *Collectanea* 40 (1978) 278.

languages can easily become a source of misunderstanding. Two weeks later Fr. Charles received another letter, this one from Dom James himself, who stated that there was no question of Fr. Louis going to Europe, especially since he was going to become a hermit.

This storm of misunderstanding left Fr. Charles somewhat dazed. Then when he received a letter from Merton himself in September begging him to: "*Please* remove my name from the Board. . . . I ask you this as a favour,"[18] it was more than clear that Merton's presence at the meeting was out of the question. From his hermitage Merton had written in that same letter: "The magazine can do much for the Order. I think the problems of the American houses are only just beginning. In ten years from now I think we will have a different picture of the Order in the United States." This was a prophetic statement, but he could have said not only the Order in the United States, but the Order as a whole. What Fr. Charles retained most from this episode, and what he likes to repeat with a bit of pride, is that he was instrumental in Thomas Merton's being permitted to become a hermit. Merton himself intimated this to Fr. Charles: "As a matter of fact, I think that it is due to your invitation (to Scourmont) that I am now out of the novitiate and in the hermitage."[19] In another letter to Fr. Charles shortly afterward, Merton reflected on enclosure and Cistercian observance in general:

> When I first came here, and up until about ordination, I was a very hard line *strictioris observantiae* Trappist. After ordination I had enough sickness and problems to learn a wiser way of being a monk and I think I have learned by experience that the absolutist viewpoint is—as you know and as any real monk knows—often just an excuse for self-love and defiance of God. More and more I see that there is nothing but submission to God, as directly and as inscrutably as He may will it.[20]

18. "The Cistercian . . ." (Letter of September 13, 1965) 327.
19. Ibid. (Letter of September 13, 1965) 327.
20. Ibid. (Letter of September 18, 1965) 328.

This letter and Fr. Charles' reply to it show how well the two monks understood each other as a result of their own personal experiences. After telling Fr. Louis that the *Collectanea* meeting—with ten participants: two abbots, two definitors and six other monks—had taken place, and that Dom Samson (James) Wicksteed would be the editor of the new American-English edition of the magazine, he explained that it would not be a simple translation of *Collectanea*. The best articles in each magazine would appear in the other, although not in the same issues. There would be one single *Bulletin* for both. After more shop talk, Fr. Charles concluded as a friend:

> I realize very well the difficulties in your life. But I pray God that bitterness of heart will not come near your cell. My twenty-five years of monastic life have left me with one single word: *patientissime* (the only superlative in the *Rule*), and this means in regard to God as well as to our fellow men. If a monk loses this, the salt he is supposed to be on earth perishes.[21]

Correspondence continued between the two monks. Then, a little over two years later, Father Charles found himself in an airplane with Merton's Father Immediate on his way to Gethsemani for the election of the new abbot. In its own way Providence had arranged for the two monks to meet.

Dumont discovers America

On the feast of the Epiphany, in the guesthouse suite where he lodged during his stay at Gethsemani Abbey, Fr. Charles wrote to Dom Guerric:

> The trip was very easy . . . We were supposed to spend the night in New York and continue the next morning, but in this country the faster the better. The chaplain at the airport, Msgr. Fox (no relation to Dom James), was waiting to tell

21. C. Dumont, letter to Thomas Merton, Sept. 18, 1965.

> us that we should take a connecting flight for Louisville immediately at La Guardia airport. It is possible to go from one airport to the other in a quarter of an hour if you take a helicopter, and in half an hour by car . . . we had a race in a taxi . . . like in a western movie. The jet for Louisville was waiting for us. Another hour and a half and the thousand kilometers which separate Louisville from New York were covered in a flap of a wing. Dom James, smiling as always, was waiting for us with his brother, and in an hour—through the forest covered with snow—we were at Gethsemani. It was 10 p.m. (local time), but 4 a.m. at Scourmont. If it is horribly cold outside (–15C), it is terribly hot inside . . . This morning I concelebrated and it was the most beautiful liturgy I have ever attended. The church has recently been completely renovated. Extremely simple. (1.6.68)

While Fr. Charles was at Gethsemani, Dom James invited him to speak in chapter one evening, and on another occasion he spoke to the junior professed. The day before the election he had an opportunity to visit Louisville and Lexington. He found the blue-grass countryside splendid, with its race horse farms and forests. He wrote to his abbot: "I have bought a hat, because when I visited a family here the lady exclaimed in surprise: 'The priest with a beret!' I thought it was time to do so, to be like other people" (1.15.68).

The abbots of Holy Spirit and New Clairvaux (Gethsemani's daughter-houses), present for the election, both invited Fr. Charles to come to their monasteries. He already knew Dom Eusebius of New Clairvaux, in California, because when Dom Eusebius was a student in Rome he had spent some of his vacation time at Scourmont. It was Fr. Charles who had taken him to visit the ruins of the famous Abbey of Villers in Brabant. Now, when the Belgian monk modestly hesitated to accept the abbots' invitations because he had not brought any lecture notes with him, he was told simply: "Just bring your brains."[22]

It was while he was at breakfast one morning that Fr. Charles saw Merton for the first time. He looked up and there he was, clad

22. C. Dumont, letter to Dom Guerric, January 15, 1968.

in overalls, standing in the doorway. Merton had come up to the monastery for some provisions. From then on Fr. Charles spoke with Merton for a while each day, and after the election of Fr. Flavian Burns as Gethsemani's new abbot he spent an afternoon with his friend at his hermitage. After years of personal and even intimate correspondence, neither of the two monks knew exactly how to describe his impressions of this first encounter with the other. Fr. Charles wrote simply to his abbot: "We understand each other marvelously! What a unique man! . . . I spent the afternoon at his hermitage, drinking awful canned beer" (1.15-17.68).[23] For a Belgian, and especially for a monk from a monastery that operates a well-known brewery, what could be worse than canned beer!

Fr. Charles enjoyed his stay at Gethsemani. As it happened, however, an epidemic of flu was raging in the community and of course Fr. Charles caught it, and bronchitis as well. Still, his desire to see monastic life as it is lived in American houses was stronger than the flu. While at Gethsemani he had received more invitations to visit other monasteries in the United States, so that after a few days of rest he wrote to his abbot to give him his itinerary: Spencer, Genesee, New Melleray, Guadalupe, Vina and Redwoods. Dom Guerric's mind must have been reeling as he read on: "But that's not all! Dom Augustine Moore, of Holy Spirit, has invited me to make 'a little detour' to Conyers" (1.15.68). After that he would visit Mepkin and Berryville. Then on the way home he would pass by New York, but unfortunately not at the right time to see the Saint Patrick's Day parade. What was originally intended to be a short visit to North America was turning into to a three-month journey! In other words, Fr. Charles was about to set out upon a *grand tour* of the United States.

After leaving Gethsemani, the starting point was New York. There he was met by the brother of a Caldey monk, who showed him some of the sights. A brother of Fr. Basil Pennington then picked him up and drove him to Spencer, where he was impressed by the beautiful monastery and found the brothers to be a very

23. Actually, Fr. Charles spent two afternoons with Merton at his hermitage.

stimulating audience. One day a monk drove him to Wrentham to speak to the nuns. He particularly enjoyed the question period which followed his talk there. His next stop was Genesee. From his seat next to the window on the plane from Boston to Rochester he enjoyed the view of Lake Ontario and upstate New York.

At Genesee, a smaller community than Spencer, he was given a room in the infirmary because, as he wrote to Dom Guerric, "the guesthouse is two kilometers away and I don't know how to drive" (2.1.68). At New Melleray he was welcomed by Dom David Wechter, whom he remembered well from Rome where they had played tennis together in 1952. Everywhere he went he was impressed by the beauty of the country and the variety of the scenery. In Iowa, the sweeping expanses of farm country covered with rich crops charmed him while from the plane he watched corn being cut. He wrote to Dom Guerric that if he would buy one of those corn-cutting machines he would cut all of Scourmont's corn by himself.

The flight from Chicago to the West Coast gave him another opportunity to experience the vastness of the United States. One impression which grew as he went from monastery to monastery was how different the houses were from one another. He was also very glad to find comfortable guesthouse quarters everywhere. These accommodations helped him to avoid excessive fatigue and consequently to stave off another attack of his illness which was always lurking in the shadows.

The West Coast communities: Guadalupe, Vina and Redwoods, made a very good impression on Fr. Charles. He wished Scourmont's Brother Théophile could see the bookbindery at Guadalupe, and the way the New Clairvaux monks harvested the prunes in their vast orchards astonished him. He was thrilled, of course, by the spectacular scenery along the dramatic Oregon coast and by the sequoias in California. (Be it said in passing that at Scourmont, too, there is a giant sequoia in the courtyard between the guesthouse and the monastery.)

It was while he was at Redwoods that fatigue from this marathon finally caught up with Fr. Charles. For several days he was quite sick so that he was obliged to cancel his visits to

Holy Trinity and Snowmass, the next two monasteries on his itinerary. Fully aware that he could not hope for a complete cure of his intestinal illness, and that the only remedy was complete rest—doing nothing!—his morale sank. He stayed at Redwoods for a week or so, in solitude and watching the timid sun filter through the towering trees. Gradually, as his strength returned his spirits rose. Several monasteries remained on his itinerary: Holy Spirit, Mepkin and Berryville, so after a brief halt at San Francisco, which he considered to be the most beautiful city in the United States, he departed for Atlanta.

Fr. Charles felt quite at ease at Holy Spirit, "perhaps because it is southern; after all, I have a southerner complex myself"[24] (3.14.68), but also because of the quality of the community. It was the abbot of Holy Spirit, Dom Augustine, who himself drove Fr. Charles on from Conyers to Mepkin. Afterwards, when speaking of this trip, Fr. Charles would say with amazement: "A six-hour drive, and the abbot said, 'It's not far!' " By then he had begun to realize the different conceptions of distances Americans and Europeans have. After his visit to Mepkin, Fr. Charles took a plane for New York and two days later returned to Belgium . . . "the end of my *grand tour* and my gyrovagery" (3.14.68).

On arrival his first stop was Louvain, for a checkup by his doctor. When that was over Fr. Charles returned to Scourmont. Once settled at home again, he reminisced about the rather extraordinary trip he had just completed. It was, in fact, the first time that a European monk had spoken to the American communities about the Cistercian Fathers. He had been very touched by the warm welcome he received everywhere, and by the way the monks and nuns had received what he had to say about the Cistercian heritage. Many things he had seen and experienced impressed him deeply, so that the editor of *Collectanea* chose to share his reflections about his trip with the readers of the magazine. They were published in *Chroniques des Monastères,* a supplement to the last issue of 1968. The following lines are taken from this chronicle:

24. Fr. Charles was referring to the demarcation between Flemish and Wallon in Belgium.

It is not enough to say on either side of the Atlantic: "They are very different from us!" We have to accept this, consciously and willingly, and even discover some advantages in this fact. Long before modern sociologists, La Bruyère wrote: "It seems to me that a person's spirit, humor, passions, tastes and sentiments depend on the place he or she comes from" *(Les caractères. Du coeur).* If generalizations are dangerous when we talk about this Union of 50 "countries," there are nevertheless some common characteristics. These have been carved by a common experience of conquest of territory, an experience all the more intense because it was condensed within an extremely short period of time. This contrast between the geographical and historical dimensions is at the origin of more than one disconcerting aspect of the American spirit, of the *American way of life.* To know men, one must live with them in their daily life. No matter how much we desire unity of the Order, nothing can be done about the fact that people are born French, Japanese or American, and not Benedictine or Cistercian. In spite of a common ideal, differences have to be respected and this is possible only by mutual efforts to understand others. The first obstacle to surmount is language. Instead of making communication easier, interpreters sometimes blur things. So much contempt—sometimes very serious—is due to translations that have to be made quickly and lack nuances.

The recent decrease of personnel has been as abrupt as its increase was after World War II; all the monasteries have experienced this hard turn of events. But there, in America, a problem is not a theme for metaphysical meditation but an obstacle to be overcome. Means are being sought everywhere to remedy this crisis.

The formation of the monks is no doubt a weak point, as the reports of their regional meetings state. Formation for reading and study especially, but it should be remembered that teaching and research methods in American universities are almost the direct opposite of *lectio divina.* This type of formation which leaves room for freedom is paradoxically quite difficult because, if the prevailing conformity in our Order which has resulted from a certain system of observances has been able to produce saints it has also hindered the progressive evolution of the Institution. Superiors feel at a loss when faced with . . . the "creativity" of the younger generation, notably that of young monks who have returned after studying in a university and because of lack of previous formation have not been able to readjust . . . But difficulties are stimulating in the land of the astronauts, so that more than elsewhere, and because of their particular problems, the monks pool their energy to seek common ways of renewal in the Church and in the Order. It is not a question of timid mitigations, but of being a monk and keeping abreast of the times. We can count on them to take interesting initiatives, because—except when they feel they are bound by a law—few people are less inhibited than they when it comes to obsolete things from the past. American hospitality: Material comfort is only a small part of it, because the pleasant surprise is a cordial and warm welcome, open and free from personal or social judgments which in our (European) countries are almost instinctive. . . . Guests are received in the monastic guesthouses in a particularly fraternal and attentive way. Their retreats for men give the monks real influence, but they could be more open, in the way Fr. Merton meant. He himself was a good example of monastic outreach . . . It would be a form of monastic apostolate which would be a service at this time of crisis which is shaking the Church, and even in the spiritual evolution of America in search for itself today.

Work in American monasteries . . . As mechanized as their work may be, it is here that the most tenacious European prejudices fall apart. Americans have a surprisingly detached attitude toward technical progress . . . They are not attached to their machines or their *gadgets.* The machine is useful; they use it, that's all . . . (Jacques) Maritain said that what Americans expect from their visitors is approval, encouragement, intellectual reassurance. This does not exclude, but presupposes, critical advice which they listen to with disarming humility. And what they always offer is new hope. Our (American) monasteries, in spite of present difficulties and the number of monks who have

> left, are brimming over with vitality, and give solid reasons for hope to monks of the Old World, who also have great need of them.[25]

After his return from the United States Fr. Charles was busy preparing the coming issues of *Collectanea*. The second, on the theme *Charisme et codification,* included some pertinent articles on law, which had become one of the principal topics under discussion in the Order. The last issue that year was once again on formation, more specifically on *Renewal of Monastic Formation,* with the lead-off article by Thomas Merton.[26]

In the hands of a surgeon

Then, what had been threatening Fr. Charles for a long time happened. He suddenly became very ill and had to be rushed to the hospital at Louvain. Because of the French-Flemish language situation in Belgium, this time he was hospitalized at Saint Pierre Clinic (French-speaking) rather than Saint Raphael Clinic (Flemish-speaking) where he had been treated before. This involved transfer of records and other red tape. The change also meant that Fr. Charles had a new doctor, one who decided to perform an intestinal operation on his monk-patient without delay.

After it was over Dom Guerric was at his side as Fr. Charles slowly came out of the anesthesia. His eyes were open but he was not yet fully conscious, so that he just lay there staring blankly at Dom Guerric. When a nurse came in and saw this she turned to Dom Guerric and said with perplexity, "Does he *know* you?" Dom Guerric assured her that he did.

After this gruelling experience, by August thirteenth Fr. Charles had recovered sufficiently to be able to write a letter to his abbot and brother monks:

25. C. Dumont, Supplement to *Collectanea* 30 (1968) fasc. 3 & 4, 1–4.

26. "Renouveau de la formation monastique." This article had already appeared under the title "Renewal in Monastic Education," in *Cistercian Studies* III (1968) 247–252.

> Dear Father Abbot and my dear Brothers,
> These are the first words I have written (since my operation), and I am writing them clandestinely, because the nurse, Sr. X., has forbidden me to write . . . But I want to wish you a happy feast day (of the Assumption) and thank you with all my heart for your prayers . . . There is no need to bore you with anatomical details. I have been told that I was fortunate to have had the operation after already having this disease two years, because that way they could take out a piece of the tube 60 centimeters long, whereas when a person is operated on at the onset of the disease only a little piece is taken out and later they have to start over again several times. . . . I think that, on this August 15th feast day, my recent adventure gives me something to reflect on because with the Assumption of the Blessed Virgin the whole mystery of the Redemption and the transfiguration of our body is put before us for meditation. In spite of the Platonism of the Fathers, Saint Bernard—himself often ill—always considered his valiant body as his soul's best companion, a companion which he did not seem to want very much to leave . . . except for a little while . . . because he could not imagine how a man could ever be perfectly happy without his body . . . I can assure you that during what I have lived through recently, koinonia—fraternity—is not an empty word, and that if the length and topography of my *viscera misericordiae* have changed, they are still in the right place. (8.13.68)

After a month of convalescence at Soleilmont, Fr. Charles returned to Scourmont at the beginning of October. He had not yet completely recovered, however, so Dom Guerric sent him to Caldey for a while in the hope that the bracing air on the Island would do him good. Fr. Charles passed a month there, pleased to have the company of Peter Anson, who was at Caldey for a visit.[27] It was the first time he had met Anson. Every few days Fr. Charles mailed a report on his health to Dom Guerric, and

27. Peter Anson, who had been a monk at Caldey, wrote an account of happenings on the island during the period preceding the community's entering the Catholic Church.

he spent three hours each day walking around the island, accompanied by the monks' dog Leah who "ran around a lot, and all over the place" (10.12.68).

While he was still at Caldey, he received an invitation from Fr. Basil Pennington to a Symposium on the Cistercian Spirit to be held at Spencer in February, 1969, but he did not feel up to accepting it. Also, at that moment he was anxious to return to Scourmont and get back to his work on *Collectanea*. Fr. Patrick Catry had been appointed cellarer at Mont-des-Cats and had to give up editing the *Bulletin*, so Fr. Charles would have to take care of it himself at least temporarily.

Death of Thomas Merton

In December came the devastating news of Thomas Merton's death during the Monastic Congress in Bangkok. As one could expect, both *Collectanea* and *Cistercian Studies* paid tribute to the Gethsemani monk-author in their next issue. In addition to Dom Flavian's homily at Fr. Louis' funeral Mass and several texts by Merton himself, *Collectanea* published Dom Jean Leclercq's account of Merton's participation at the Bangkok Congress which ended with the last words of Merton's final lecture: "So I will disappear." Fr. Charles himself wrote the introduction to this issue of *Collectanea: Père Louis–Thomas Merton,* but what a difficult task it was to write about this monk whose death had been even more enigmatic than his life!

> (Merton) continually sought to escape from any kind of identification . . . He differed, evolved, changed frequently, and that sometimes upset certain people. Alone, he held the threads of an unexpressed synthesis. He sought this desperately, finally convinced that it is to be found over and above philosophy and psychology, in an intuition we sometimes experience as emptiness, and which constitutes the plenitude of someone who no longer disposes of himself . . . Merton died just when many of his ideas were beginning to be accepted in the Order . . . If he was somewhat of a prophet, and sometimes

as vehement as Jonas, he was well aware (and we, no doubt, even more than he) that he owed it to the time he spent in the darkness of the belly of the whale. . . . Father Louis excelled in the monastic virtue of friendship. He practiced it especially in his letters, a form of art current in the Middle Ages which modern means of communication have caused to disappear. He expressed himself more freely with his pen because, as he once admitted to me, he was timid when he found himself face to face with his visitors. He had discovered this quality of monastic friendship in our ancient writers.

Thomas Merton was a true heir of the Cistercian spiritual authors . . . Those who truly continue in their lineage are those who, like them, know how to transmit in the style and language of their time a message of the Spirit as only a monk can grasp and present it . . . It was not always easy for him . . . It is Christ who in his love brought the two men, Thomas Merton and Father Louis, together to make only one at the end of his life.

Fr. Charles concluded his tribute to his cherished friend as follows:

Unified, he found himself in the One whom he had sought on human paths, none of which left him indifferent, but also, more surely, interiorly "in a courageous trek in silence, in a long flight by night." This story he will write no longer, nor will anyone else write it; besides, he has already forgotten it. We, however, will not forget it.[28]

In 1978, to mark the tenth anniversary of Merton's death, both *Collectanea* and *Cistercian Studies* again devoted a commemorative issue to him. Fr. Charles offered as his contribution to both magazines a number of extracts from letters Fr. Louis had written to him, together with his own comments on them.[29] "As I reread these letters," he wrote, "and recall these memories, the charm of his presence and friendship come back to me

28. C. Dumont, "Père Louis–Thomas Merton," *Collectanea* 31 (1969) 3–7.

29. C. Dumont, "The Cistercian beneath the Surface," *Cistercian Studies* 13 (1978) 325–332 and "Lettres au rédacteur des *Collectanea:* 1953–1968." *Collectanea* 40 (1978) 275–286.

. . ."[30] This friendship between the Gethsemani monk and the Scourmont monk had prompted Merton to write a poem for Fr. Charles—one of his few poems in French—entitled *Le Secret*. Fr. Charles commented on it as follows:

> He once sent me a charmingly naïve poem, written in short French verses one spring morning. The point was *The Secret* of spiritual presence: "Do not seek to see me, I shall be there without knowing, nameless, faceless, nowhere, everywhere . . . nobody, everybody . . . naked heart . . . in the deep night. . . ."[31]

In the same issue of the magazine Fr. Charles' ten-years-later reply to *The Secret* was his poem *"Quel est ton visage?"*[32]

Quel est ton visage?

Tu n'étais plus personne
Au monde oblitéré
Pour qui ce glas qui sonne
Sur ton corps enterré?

Le vent t'identifie
Fuyant dans les bouleaux.
L'amour te sacrifie
Consentant comme l'eau.

Dans sa robe de laine
Le koan de ton nom
Erre encore sur la plaine
Où tu murmurais: "Non!"

Humble refus sacré
Assoiffé d'amplitude
En son écrin nacré
De vide plenitude.

Which is your face ?

You were no longer anyone
In the obliterated world
For whom is the bell tolling
Over your buried body?

The wind recognizes you
Fleeing among the birch trees.
Love sacrifices you
Consenting like water.

In its woolen robe
The koan of your name
Still roams on the plain
Where you murmured: "No!"

Sacred, humble refusal
Thirsting for wide spaces
In its mother-of-pearl jewel-box
Of empty fulness.

30. Thomas Merton. "Lettres au rédacteur des *Collectanea* 1953–1968," 275–286, here 285. See also "The Cistercian beneath the Surface," 325–332.

31. Ibid., 331.

32. This poem appeared in *Collectanea* 40 (1978) 298–299, along with the editor's correspondence with Merton quoted above.

Bangkok, Géthsemani,
Moine à l'âme profonde
Où es–tu mon ami
Qui n'étais pas au monde?

Bangkok, Gethsemani,
Monk of fathomless soul
Where are you, my friend
Who were not of this world?

Rêveur de solitude,
De plus haute attention
Et pour la multitude
Blessé de compassion.

Dreamer of solitude
In flights of lofty alertness
And for the multitude
Wounded by compassion.

Coeur pur au regard clair
Vainqueur du grand orage
Serais–tu dans l'éclair
Déchirant notre plage?

Pure heart with a clear gaze
Victor over the great storm
Are you perhaps in the lightning
Tearing our shore?

Ermite au coeur ouvert
Écris–nous ton grand songe
Pour le mettre au travers
De plus sérieux mensonge.

Hermit with open heart
Write us your great dream
To oppose it to
The most grave untruth.

Rappelle–toi le livre
Secrètement écrit,
De la peine de vivre,
Jonas, et de tes cris.

Remember the book
Secretly written,
Of the labor of living,
Jonas, and of your cries

Redis–nous l'espérance
De ton rêve ébloui
Et la marche en silence
Jusqu'à ton dernier oui.

Tell us again about the hope
Of your dazzling day-dream
And your walking on in silence
To your final yes.

Où es–tu, dans l'azur?
J'entends chanter un merle.
Ton humour le plus pur
Joue-t-il avec la Perle?

Where are you, in the blue sky?
I hear a blackbird singing.
And your humor so pure
Is it playing with the Pearl?

Thomas? Louis? Présage
Pauvre d'identité
Quel est ton vrai visage
Dans l'or du long Été?

Thomas? Louis? Poor
Foreshowing of identity
Which is your real face
In the gold of the long summer?

In 1985, while Fr. Charles was at the Bernardine nuns' convent at Charleville-Mezières for several days of ministry, he met an American scholar, Dr. Bernard Mathieu, who was in France doing research on the poet Arthur Rimbaud. Dr. Mathieu was delighted to come upon a monk who had known Thomas Merton and the two of them had a stimulating discussion on the *The Secret* and *Quel est ton visage.* When Dr. Mathieu returned home to Lewiston, Maine, he wrote an article about Fr. Charles and these poems. He saw *The Secret* as a "witty, playful, deeply affectionate and deeply visionary poem about the *secret* of the final journey which each of us takes: the journey of death."[33] Ironically, he said, it was a journey Merton himself was to make soon after writing the poem.

In his article "The Cistercian beneath the surface" Fr. Charles also quoted a long passage from Merton's circular letter to his friends at Easter 1968, because as he said:

> although (this) extract does not come from a letter addressed to me personally . . . it echoes so exactly our last conversation in his hermitage in January that it is almost a record of it without, I must say, the touch of humour and the smiles which took away from it any bitterness. We were remembering our first years in our monasteries in the forties.[34]

In that circular Merton spoke about the contradictions a monk can meet up with in the monastic life, and marvelled that in spite of them he was still in the monastery:

> It would be utterly dishonest for me to claim that when I first came to Gethsemani the place was not for me a "sign of Christ." It *was,* in spite of all the shortcomings I instinctively realized . . . On the other hand, the inhumanities of the secular life are incomparably worse (so we feel) even though they may to some seem acceptably 'painless' (or even enjoyable). Thus we—I speak for myself and others like me who have stayed put in spite of the fact that we have seen good reasons not to—repeatedly renewed out initial choice. Though we have shed one illusion after another and

33. Dr. Bernard Mathieu, *"Quel est ton visage?"* in *The Church World,* Lewiston, ME (December 19, 1985) 9.

34. "The Cistercian beneath the surface," 330.

> gone deeper and deeper into the radical questioning of our life and our vocation, we have nevertheless elected to stay with it because we have continued to believe that this was what God asked of us.[35]

Is this belief not the real reason why anyone stays in a monastery? Was it not the fundamental bond between these two friends, Merton and Fr. Charles? Merton was gone, but he remained very present for Fr. Charles. During the years of great change in the Order he often referred to his friend's writings, and he was increasingly convinced of the importance of the Gethsemani monk's insights for the evolution of the Order and the development of the contemplative life, not only among monks and nuns, but also among numberless lay people seeking God.

Although Fr. Charles had regained relatively good health since his operation, he realized that he was not really cured. He continued to suffer from the same disease, but now at least it was more bearable. This was both encouraging and fortunate, because the coming year was to be a busy one for him. In January he shared his impressions of the American monasteries in a talk to the monks of Mont–des–Cats. Toward Easter he was elected for a four-year term as a member of the pastoral Council for the diocese of Tournai, as well as secretary of the regional Council of Thudinie. And in May he was invited to the Benedictine Abbeys of St André–lez–Bruges and Bethany (Loppem) for several lectures on Kierkegaard, whose works continued to interest him as much as they had when he was a young student in philosophy. And strange as it may seem, during the next two years he also taught religion to the older girls at the Lycée at Pesche, not far from Scourmont.

An International Ecumenical Meeting

In July, 1969, an International Ecumenical Meeting took place at Ramegnies–Chin, near Tournai. This meeting, which brought

35. Ibid., 330–331.

together a number of outstanding persons of various religions, had been organized by Fr. Maur, who was at that time a member of the diocesan ecumenical secretariat. Fr. Charles was not originally scheduled to participate, but when Fr. Henri de Lubac fell ill and was unable to attend Fr. Maur asked his confrere to substitute for him and to speak about Merton. Later, with an amused little smile Fr. Charles would enjoy telling how he had "replaced Fr. de Lubac." The title he chose for his lecture was: *Thomas Merton, a Contemplative at the Heart of the World*.[36] In it he showed how Merton had succeeded in uniting action and contemplation in his monastic life. Among the participants at the meeting were a number of persons whom Fr. Charles knew already, such as Taizé's Frère Pierre–Yves Emery and Fr. Nicholas Egender, prior of Chevetogne. Other participants he met for the first time: the Roumanian Orthodox monk Anthony Plâmâdealâ, Mgr. Antoine Bloom, Youakin Moubarac, the poet Pierre Emmanuel and Sr. Eileen Mary, of the Anglican Benedictine community of Fairacres, Oxford, to mention just a few.

After this meeting Fr. Charles went directly to the monastery of the Benedictine nuns at Ermeton for another colloquium, because as editor of *Collectanea* he had to be abreast of everything that was happening in monastic circles. Meetings were also scheduled during the coming year for the collaborators of the *Bulletin de Spiritualité Monastique.* Later, Fr. Charles returned to Mont–des–Cats to give lectures on Saint Bernard. It was the first time he had given a series of lectures on the Abbot of Clairvaux. It would not be the last!

Since the 1967 General Chapter Fr. Charles had been working on new Constitutions for the Order in a more or less informal way, but he had not become really involved in this study. He had missed a meeting of the Constitutions Committee because of his trip to America in 1968, but felt that what he had learned from his visits

36. This article first appeared in French as "Recherche oecuménique: prière et action," ed. C.D.D., Tournai; an English translation appeared in *Lumen Vitae* 24 (1969) 4. Reprinted in *Thomas Merton Monk, a Monastic Tribute*. Ed. Patrick Hart, ocso (NY: Sheed & Ward, 1974). 'The Contemplative,' 125–139.

to the U.S. houses was more valuable for his work on the Constitutions than the meeting would have been. The 1969 General Chapter set up a new Law Commission with Dom Guerric as president, and composed of the following members: Fr. Maur (secretary), Dom Vincent Hermans, procurator general, Fr. Edmund Mikkers (Achel), Dom Sergio Del Pino Campos (Cardena), Fr. Basil Pennington (Spencer), Fr. Charles and two other abbots to be chosen from the American and Spanish regions.

In February, 1973, a meeting of the Law Commission was held at Scourmont. On the agenda were certain questions referred to the Commission by the First General Chapter of Abbesses which had taken place at Rome, in September, 1971. One of them concerned nuns' chaplains. With the changes that were coming about in the Order at that time it seemed that the roles of both the chaplain and the abbess in the area of spiritual direction were also changing. One question that came up was: Who should be responsible for spiritual direction in monasteries of nuns: the abbess? the chaplain? both? Though the two aspects of the question were distinct they were related—as the Minutes of the Law Commission Meeting indicated—, but before a nuanced reply could be given a number of factors had to be taken into account: differences from one monastery or region to another, masculine and feminine psychology, role of the priesthood in spiritual direction, conception of a masculine and a feminine community, etc. The Commission decided that a survey should be made. Fr. Charles was asked to contact chaplains and some former chaplains, and Sr. Michael (later Elizabeth), a nun correspondent of the Law Commission designated by the Chapter of Abbesses, was to contact the abbesses.[37] This survey was carried out by means of a questionnaire and resulted in a very rich dossier which served as the basis for a document entitled *The Role of the Chaplain and Spiritual Direction of Cistercian Nuns*, communicated to the communities of the Order.

37. *Minutes* of the Meeting of the Law Commission, Scourmont (January 17–21, 1972) 4. Document CC–72/1.

4

TRANSMITTING THE CISTERCIAN CHARISM

I must say that my own knowledge of Saint Bernard is becoming very unified. I am convinced that his theology is built around the mystery of the Incarnation, and also his monastic spirituality. I discover beauty and truths which give me joy and great assurance in our vocation.

C. D.

So far Fr. Charles had lectured occasionally in various monasteries in Europe and North America and had participated in a number of monastic colloquies. From 1971 on he began to receive an increasing number of invitations to speak to communities about the Cistercian Fathers and the monastic life in general, so that in the future a large part of his time and energy was devoted to giving series of lectures and retreats in Cistercian and Benedictine monasteries in Europe and North America, and serving as a resource person at workshops for monks and/or nuns responsible for formation. He was also invited as an expert to several Regional Conferences and to the 1974 General Chapter. As we follow him through these years, we will try to bring out the major aspects of his teaching.

The period after Vatican II was turbulent in both the Church and the monastic life. In reaction to the many maverick ideas that were surfacing just about everywhere, many Cistercian communities felt the need to orient their life according to the solid doctrine of the Cistercian Fathers. Fr. Charles' own love for Cistercian spirituality consequently made his teaching all the more meaningful, especially to young monks and nuns who were eager for what was authentic. In certain monasteries he visited, in addition to his talks to the community as a whole he met with the juniors and novices, answered their questions and encouraged them to read and study the Fathers.

The Oka Symposium

In 1971 Fr. Basil Pennington organized another Cistercian Symposium. This one, on the theme of Contemplative Community, was to be held at the end of August at Notre-Dame du Lac Abbey, Oka, Quebec. Fr. Basil had been disappointed that Fr. Charles had been unable to attend the first two Symposia, at Spencer and Conyers, and wanted very much for him to give a lecture at the Oka meeting. Since his health was fairly satisfactory at this time Fr. Charles accepted the invitation, pleased with the prospect of returning to North America. Among the numerous scholars present at the Oka Symposium were Fr. Valentine Walgrave, Sr. Benedicta Ward, Dom Jean Leclercq, Fr. Chrysogonus Waddell and Dom Armand Veilleux. Fr. Charles was impressed by this Symposium: the talks and discussions were learned and instructive and the atmosphere at Oka was very pleasant. His paper, "Seeking God in Community according to Saint Aelred," was published first in *Cistercian Studies*, then reprinted in the Cistercian Publications volume *Contemplative Community, a Symposium*.[1]

1. C. Dumont, "Seeking God in Community according to Saint Aelred," *Cistercian Studies* VI (1971) 289–317. Reprinted in *Contemplative Community, a Symposium* (Washington, DC: Consortium Press, 1972) 115–149, and appeared in French as "Chercher Dieu dans la communauté selon Aelred de Rievaulx," *Collectanea* 34 (1972) 8–35.

As a result of his conversations with various participants, before the end of the meeting Fr. Charles had made changes in his travel plans. He had already visited the two other Cistercian monasteries in Quebec, Saint Romuald and Mistassini, before coming to Oka. Now he decided not to return to England for the Oxford Patristic Congress as he had originally intended, but to visit several monasteries in the United States in reply to invitations he had received during the Symposium.

So it was that on September 15 he found himself on a flight from Chicago to Dubuque on his way to New Melleray. The plane was flying low over the immense farms of the Corn Belt and, just as three years earlier, he took great pleasure in contemplating the country. While in Iowa he also visited Our Lady of the Mississippi Abbey, and then went on to Gethsemani where with great emotion he visited Thomas Merton's grave and celebrated the Eucharist in his hermitage. He also visited the Benedictine monastery of Mount Saviour in upstate New York. Brother David Steindl-Rast, a member of the Mount Saviour community, had been one of the participants at the Oka Symposium and during those few days he and Fr. Charles had discovered that they had many things in common. Brother David had seized the opportunity to ask him to come to Mount Saviour to help his community with a project concerning its periodical: *Monastic Studies*.

The Interreligious Symposium at Mount Saviour

Before returning to Belgium Fr. Charles received an invitation to come back to Mount Saviour the following year for another Symposium, this time an Interreligious monastic meeting. Brother David, who was the director of a Center of religious research for exchange on the various great spiritual traditions, had organized this meeting on the theme: Word out of silence. His aim was to bring together spiritual masters associated with the Mount Saviour Center so that they might compare their formation methods and share their experiences with superiors of monastic communities, monks and nuns, and also young lay people. Ever since the

Tournai ecumenical colloquium, and through his correspondence with Thomas Merton for *Collectanea* about monks of diverse religious traditions, Fr. Charles' interest in intermonastic dialogue had grown. The fact that so many young people seeking their way were going to India and practicing techniques taken from oriental religions made such dialogue all the more important.

When this symposium opened in August, 1972, one hundred and fifty people were present, including Raimund Panikkar and Kallistos Ware, as well as bright lights of Orthodoxy, Buddhism and Hinduism. But it was the Zen master, Josu Sasaki Rôshi who perhaps made the greatest impression on Fr. Charles. After this remarkable gathering he wrote a short chronicle on it, entitled *Le staretz et le guru*,[2] for the French periodical *La Vie Spirituelle*. Speaking from the point of view of a Christian monk, he observed that we cannot approach the "over and above everything" which all religions seek unless we remain faithful to our own tradition.[3] Not surprisingly, he concluded his chronicle by quoting from the last part of Thomas Merton's lecture at the Bangkok Monastic Congress the very morning before he died. Speaking of how openness to the great Asian traditions can shed light on our traditions, Merton had said:

> I believe that by openness to Buddhism, to Hinduism, and to these great Asian traditions, we stand a wonderful chance of learning more about the potentiality of our own traditions . . . The combination of the natural techniques and the graces and the other things that have been manifested in Asia and the Christian liberty of the gospel should bring us all at last to that full and transcendent liberty which is beyond mere cultural differences and mere externals—and mere this or that.[4]

2. C. Dumont, "Le Guru et le Staretz," *La Vie Spirituelle* 127, No. 594 (1973) 153–156.

3. Ibid., 155.

4. *The Asian Journal of Thomas Merton* (New York: New Directions, 1975) 343.

Studies for nuns: The 1972 Chimay Trimester

After a lecture by Fr. Charles at Saint Romuald before the Oka Symposium, during a conversation with one of the sisters the subject of a course of study for nuns had come up. Though such a project seemed little more than a dream at the time, in his next letter to Dom Guerric Fr. Charles mentioned it to him. As it happened, the first General Chapter of Abbesses took place almost directly after the Symposium and at this Chapter formation surfaced as one of the most urgent concerns of the abbesses. They realized that the future of the Order depended largely on the spiritual and doctrinal formation of its members. More particularly, the need for unified formation in the Order was also felt, formation solidly founded on traditional Benedictine-Cistercian spirituality. Dom Guerric, who was present at this Chapter as an abbot observer, spoke to some of the abbesses about what Fr. Charles had written him concerning a course. The proposal drew their interest and gradually the idea began to take form. Notre-Dame de la Paix Abbey, at Chimay, Belgium—just a few miles from Scourmont—seemed like an ideal place for such a project. The community of La Paix whose history goes back to the ancient Abbey of Gomerfontaine (founded in 1266) was small, but the monastery was sufficiently spacious to receive a group of about fifteen nuns. The Abbess and community of Chimay offered their hospitality and collaboration. At that time Fr. Charles was nonresident chaplain at Chimay and Fr. Maur Standaert, the prior at Scourmont, was secretary for formation for the Central/ North Europe region. All the essential factors gradually came together so that from September 28 until December 16, 1972, the first ever Patristic-Cistercian Trimester was held at Notre-Dame de la Paix.

The participants at the trimester (17 nuns from 8 different countries, including three nuns of La Paix) attended lectures in the morning, helped with common work in the afternoon and led a normal monastic life with the nuns of the community, so that there was maximum integration of study and monastic life. The program drawn up by Fr. Maur was built on a central theme: *The Image of God in Church Tradition.* Though the presentation of this theme extended from Scripture to Vatican II, the result was in no way a smattering of knowledge but followed the coherent and unified thread of the continuity of Tradition. The list of lecturers included monks, nuns and university professors. To mention only a few: Fr. Edmund Mikkers, OCSO, Fr. Gaëtano Raciti, OCSO, Canon Jean Châtillon and Sr. Gabriel Peters, OSB. A number of lectures were also given by Fr. Maur, Fr. Charles and Br. Gabriel Ghislain, of Scourmont. At least one of these three monks was present at each lecture and their availability to the students for assistance in their personal study contributed considerably to the success of the trimester.

Several times a week Fr. Maur arrived in the morning with a suitcase full of books from Scourmont's library on the subjects being studied, so that the sisters could familiarize themselves with the best classic and current works on each subject presented. Each student chose a project which she began work on during the trimester and was to continue after her return to her monastery. Fr. Charles remained at Chimay during most of the trimester. Most days he gave a short homily at the Eucharist, often relating the subject matter being studied to the day's liturgy. Besides his lectures on Saint Irenaeus, Clement of Alexandria, Saint Thomas Aquinas and, of course, Aelred of Rievaulx, he also gave extracurricular talks on contemporary philosophy and monastic theology,[5] and moderated question periods on current theological and monastic topics. Several collateral talks were also offered during the trimester, and turned out to be directly in the line of the theme. The exarch of the Patriarchate of Moscow for Western Europe, Msgr. Anthony Bloom, spoke on the Church in Russia; Fr. Charles gave an account of the Mount Saviour Symposium,[6] and the Prioress of the Olivetan Benedictine nuns of Moustiers-en-Fagnes, well-known for her iconography, explained

5. For example, "Réflexions sur la théologie monastique contemporaine," unpublished.

6. "À propos du Symposium de Mont-Saviour et du Monachisme," unpublished.

how she went about her work and invited the students to visit her convent studio near Chimay.

The results of this trimester were remarkably positive. After the nun students returned to their monasteries shortly before Christmas, most of them were asked by their abbesses to prepare classes on Patrology or the Cistercian Fathers for their sisters. In a chronicle on the trimester Sr. Anne Saword—a nun of Stapehill who as editor of *Cistercian Studies* was living at Chimay at that time—used the expression: "the University of Chimay."[7] It was in fact just that, but adapted to Cistercian life, with an open, receptive monastic and contemplative approach.[8]

Fr. Charles' health held up quite well during the trimester, so that in early January he was able to go to La Paix-Dieu to give the annual retreat and some lectures to the sisters of this new, small ecumenical community in Cévennes. Sr. Monique, of the Paix-Dieu, had been one of the students at the trimester.

Lecture tours in North America and in Europe

When Fr. Charles returned to Scourmont after several weeks in the south there remained only about a month before his next departure for North America. During his previous trip to the United States an understanding had been reached with the American abbots that both he and Fr. Edmund Mikkers would visit the monasteries in the United States within the next two years, each of them visiting monasteries in the west one year and those in the east the other year. In 1973 it was Fr. Charles' turn to lecture in the west. The secretary for formation of the American region prepared for the students a booklet of texts which would be commented on during the lectures.

After landing in Chicago Fr. Charles went first to New Melleray and Our Lady of the Mississippi, and from there on to Snow-

7. Anne Saword, "The University of Chimay," *Cistercian Studies* VIII (1973) 82–85.

8. Cf. Sr. Guénolé and Sr. Michaël, "Patristic Cistercian Trimester," *Monastic Exchange* 5, 1 (Spring, 1973) 15–19.

mass (where he was constantly drowsy because of the altitude), Guadalupe and Holy Trinity. After his visit to the monks in Utah, his schedule included a lecture at the Newman Club of the University of Utah in Salt Lake City. Introduced to the audience of a hundred people as "an international scholar from Belgium," he spoke to them on the subject of *Contemplation in the Western World: the Mysticism of Saint Bernard of Clairvaux* and replied to questions. During Holy Week he was at Redwoods. Then, from California he headed east to attend the Western Michigan University Medieval Congress at Kalamazoo. There, in the context of a session sponsored by the Cistercian Institute, he gave a talk on Aelred of Rievaulx's treatise *On Spiritual Friendship.* Then, after lectures at Genesee and several of the Canadian houses, he wound up his trip in Boston by a visit with a friend who was a professor at Harvard. He returned to Belgium with an impression of great vitality in the American monasteries and much promise for the future.

The pages of Fr. Charles' little notebook in which he marked the dates of his lecture engagements began to be filled up. In addition to talks promised to several Cistercian communities in northern France, his schedule included the Central/North Europe Regional Meeting at Orval, in June, to which he was invited as an expert, and the annual retreat at Ligugé in October. He had also been asked to present a paper on the Transfiguration in the writings of the Cistercian Fathers at the Oxford Symposium in September, but as it turned out he was unable to attend this meeting. One can imagine his astonishment and amusement when later, in an article in *The Tablet* on the Symposium, he found a very favorable account of a paper he had never given!

His topic at the Orval regional meeting was: *Experience in the Cistercian Discipline.*[9] The expression *experience of God,* much in vogue at that time, was frequently used in writings on the contemplative and monastic life, but because of the mystical

9. C. Dumont, "Expérience dans la discipline cistercienne," *Collectanea* 35 (1973) 157–160. Trans. "Experience in the Cistercian discipline," *Cistercian Studies* X (1975) 135–138.

currents coming from Far-East religions the interpretation of the word *experience* remained ambiguous and the meaning given to the expression was sometimes erroneous. In his talk at Orval, Fr. Charles spoke of experience as Saint Bernard and Saint Aelred presented it in their principal works on the monastic life:

> . . . not as a properly contemplative or mystical experience but as the experience of spiritual progress on the journey to God by the stages and steps of love. In his treatise *On the Love of God* Saint Bernard teaches that a person passes from one degree to the next, first by the repeated experience of one's need for God, and then by the joy found in assiduously frequenting him. Both experiences are fostered by the monastic life. The whole doctrine of the treatise *On the Steps of Humility* is based on the same experiential knowledge: first the true knowledge of self in one's poverty, then the knowledge of others by compassion and sympathy. This *social love* which widens the heart and teaches it to love was for the Cistercians the justification of the common life. In this context, the Incarnation is even considered by Saint Bernard to be God's experience of the human condition.
>
> Our authors often remind us that mystical experience is gratuitous. For example, William of St. Thierry writes that it takes place "when the Holy Spirit, who breathes where he wills, when he wills, as he wills and for whom he wills, sends his breath in this way. However, it remains in the power of man to prepare his heart constantly for it." (*The Golden Epistle* III, 251)[10]

Fr. Charles stressed that a person cannot reach God by simple techniques, but as the Fathers were fond of repeating, following Saint Paul: "by living soberly, justly and piously" (Ti 2:12). He also stressed that the Cistercians spoke discreetly and with reserve about their own spiritual experience.[11]

10. "Experience in the Cistercian Discipline" (quoting *The Golden Epistle* III, 251) 137.

11. The expression *experience of God* was being used in the U.S. also. In his talk Fr. Charles had referred to a letter in the *Mailbag* written by Fr. Timothy

This paper was very well received. One abbot called it captivating, and said that it exercised a profound influence on the whole meeting. As for the abbesses, almost all of those present invited Fr. Charles to come to speak in their monasteries. Such response seemed to indicate to him that he should try to put his ideas together, perhaps in book form. Although he thought of this often during the next year or so, he could not undertake such a project at that time. Actually, 1973 was probably not the right moment to launch such a work because the Order was still going through a period of change and experimentation. A certain degree of stability was needed for such an undertaking to be durable and appreciated. Some years later the right time did come.

Fourth lecture tour in North America

Shortly after New Year's, 1974, Fr. Charles again set out for the United States, this time to visit monasteries in the East and Middle West, as well as the two houses of nuns in Canada. His first stop was Quebec, where the weather was typical for January: lots of snow and bitterly cold. By some miracle he did not get sick.

On this trip he visited Ava, where he had a rather unique adventure. One day he went for a trek around the monastery's vast property. After walking for about two hours he came to an impasse: he found himself before a cliff alongside a wide river. He stopped and sized up the situation. He had no other choice but to climb the cliff, and by some miracle he succeeded in doing so without mishap. Once at the top he plodded on through the woods, thinking that he was probably completely lost, when suddenly he came to a clearing and saw a small cabin. As he approached it, through a little window he could see a man seated at

---

Vander Vennet, of Vina, in which he proposed that "Maybe we could shift our perspective, our thinking, from 'experiencing' and methods of spiritual experience to 'sincere searching for God' . . . Saint Benedict speaks of 'truly seeking God,' and he should know since he started this Benedictine business." *Mailbag* 13 (March 27, 1973) 3.

a table, reading from a large book. He knocked hard on the door and when the man opened it Fr. Charles realized that he was a monk. He had been occupied with his *lectio,* reading Saint John Chrysostom. A few days later, in a letter to his abbot and brothers at Scourmont Fr. Charles wrote: "The tendency (in the U.S.) toward the hermit life is a bit allayed by the use of private rooms, but I met a *real* hermit with whom I had a long conversation like the hermits in the desert of Nitria used to have" (9.21.74).

Meeting this monk did not change his opinion that, in general, the hermit life is not for Cistercians. Both Saint Bernard and Saint Aelred showed quite clearly in their teaching that community life as a way to union with God is one of the fundamental aspects of Cistercian spirituality. Still, he did admit that there can be exceptions, and the hermit-monk he had found at Ava was one of them. Not long after, in another monastery a young monk spoke to him enthusiastically about the hermit life he had begun to live: "It's wonderful! You work when you want, you eat when you want, you pray when you want." A few days later, during a lecture, Fr. Charles quoted a bit of dry humor from a sermon by Saint Aelred where the abbot of Rievaulx said that, yes, there are monks who prefer the hermit type of life because they can pray when they want, eat when they want, work when they want, etc. All at once he noticed that the face of a young monk sitting in the first row had become as red as a beet, right up to his ears. He suddenly realized that it was the young monk who had recently described his own new hermit life in the same terms!

At Genesee Fr. Stephen, the regional secretary for Formation, approached Fr. Charles about organizing a two-week seminar on Saint Aelred for monks, nuns and lay scholars. The idea attracted Fr. Charles' interest so that, when he retired to his room that evening, on a sudden inspiration he wrote out his thoughts on what such a seminar should be. These pages were published in the next issue of *Monastic Exchange* under the title: *Rationale for a Projected Seminar: Studies in Cistercian Renewal,* in which he summarized his views on Cistercian formation. The following lines taken from this paper give the guiding principles:

> The immediate purpose of these studies (i.e., Cistercian studies, and the seminar in particular) is to help us to recover, in its integral and harmonious unity, the fullness of our Cistercian way of life. To live this life as men of our time, as our fathers did in their day, we have to integrate many truths of modern anthropology as well as personal experiences of the world in which we have been educated—even though we have decided to live at a certain distance from society in accord with the fundamental principle of monastic tradition . . . We should, therefore, study in depth and detail, according to the historica-phenomenological approach, the essential and necessary means our Fathers chose and harmonized in their plan to follow the Benedictine Rule, a rule which was itself a western summary and adaptation of previous monastic tradition . . . Each successful reform witnesses a new synthesis of the two perennial elements: *praxis* and *theoria,* according to the legitimate needs of the time . . . Obviously, a great deal of modern values still need to be integrated into our efforts at aggiornamento. Too often, this latter has amounted simply to superficial modernization or *secularization*. We cannot be estranged from our time—contrary to the nineteenth century attitude which plagued us for so long. Modern phenomenology, depth psychology, and some sociology can help us to discern what can and must be assumed by our own Cistercian tradition, in order to achieve a new synthesis. The scale of values must be dictated by concern to recover the unity of our life: the condition for truth and beauty.[12]

What had been happening to *Collectanea* while Fr. Charles was touring North American monasteries? There were no problems about the magazine because during his journey he kept in touch regularly with associate editor Brother Gabriel Ghislain about articles to publish, and he himself continued to write book reviews. Still, there were other occupations and projects which required his attention.

12. C. Dumont, "Rationale for a Projected Seminar: Studies in Cistercian Renewal," *Monastic Exchange* 6, 3 (Fall, 1974) 59–61.

Expert at the 1974 General Chapter of Abbots

The proposal by the Central Europe Regional Conference that Fr. Charles should be invited to the 1974 General Chapter of Abbots at Rome was accepted by the Consilium Generale during its meeting at Viaceli. Although Fr. Charles showed little interest in juridical questions his keen mind was able to cut through the intricacies of legal discussions to discern the kernel of what was essential. This sometimes left more juridically inclined monks embarrassingly unarmed and, it must be said, exasperated. At the 1974 General Chapter he spoke at length twice in plenary session. The first time was during a discussion on liturgy, more particularly on the question of whether communities might omit one or more of the Little Hours or recite them elsewhere than in choir. As this discussion went on Fr. Charles saw different interpretations of the Rule, confusion between the law and its application and a risk of liquidating a tradition because of a practical problem of time in the monasteries. He remarked that Dom Augustin de Lestrange "had applied measures exactly the inverse of those we wish to take today. He broke up the monastic day in an inhuman fashion, and to do that he considered himself authorized to completely forget the tradition; God knows how we regret it today!"[13]

Later on in the Chapter, in the context of a proposed declaration on unity of the communities, Fr. Charles observed:

> If we wish to have consensus in our communities, and also in the General Chapter, it cannot be but with regard to the Cistercian life, seen in its unity. As the Abbot of Phare said: "Zen is a life," and we, hearing that, thought spontaneously: "Citeaux is a way of life." Recent critiques of monastic life have had the effect of disintegrating this organic unity of our life . . . One might say that on the one hand there are many things which we have adopted without being able to assimilate them, and on the other hand there are many things which we have rejected without being able to do without

13. *Minutes* of the 1974 General Chapter OCSO, 145–146.

> them. This aggiornamento has often been carried out without consideration for the health of the entire organism. To rediscover this unity, in its two principal articulations (*praxis* and *theoria*), there is only one way which seems to me to be indicated, namely, a return to the balanced synthesis realized by our Fathers. Our Fathers have hardly been cited during the Chapter, except in the discourse by the Holy Father! A better knowledge of the spirituality and of the life of our Cistercian Order would help us to take a more serene and positive view of the new synthesis which we have to realize and to disengage ourselves from recent controversies which hardly interest the young and are beginning to tire us ourselves. (*Minutes*, p. 171)

This 1974 Chapter became known as the Pastoral Chapter because the pastoral duties of the abbot came up so often in the discussions. When it was over Dom Guerric and Fr. Charles took the Rome-Calais night train for Hirson and home.

Formation Projects . . . and Constitutions

Already in 1970 the secretaries for formation for the North/ Central Europe and South France Regions had organized a two-week seminar for Cistercian novice mistresses at the monastery of La Coudre, Laval. As secretary for Central Europe, Fr. Maur was the principal architect of the program. This first venture had been such a success that four more seminars were held at Laval during the next decade. In 1974, the theme to be studied was Spiritual Paternity. This was the first Laval seminar to which Fr. Charles had been invited as a lecturer, but from that time on he was present at each one. In addition to his paper on *Spiritual Paternity in the Cistercian Tradition*,[14] he presented the

14. See "*La paternité spirituelle: séminaire pour maîtresses des novices cistercienne*," Laval: Abbaye de la Coudre, September 10–25, 1974. Mimeographed. Pages 197–208 reprinted in *Sagesse ardente*. Pain de Cîteaux 8, 3rd séries (Oka: Abbaye N.-D. du Lac, 1995) 327–346, under the title: "La paternité spirituelle dans la tradition cistercienne."

synthesis of the replies of the abbesses and chaplains to the Law Commission's survey on spiritual direction. He also devoted a large part of one of his lectures to Dante's *Paradiso,* giving as an example of spiritual guidance the way Virgil, Beatrice and Saint Bernard led Dante on his journey. As we have seen, in the *Rationale for a seminar* which Fr. Charles wrote during his recent trip to the United States he had spoken about the beauty of a unified monastic life. His lectures at Laval in 1974 are an example of how he presented this approach by the use of both poetic and philosophic texts. Some time later Brother Patrick Ryan, of Genesee, published an article in *Monastic Exchange* in which he made some comments on Dante.[15] It caught Fr. Charles' eye, and he wrote to Brother Patrick referring to the lectures he had given at the Laval Seminar. In the next issue of *Monastic Exchange* Brother Patrick shared excerpts from Fr. Charles' letter and texts, some of which are given here:

> When I was thinking over what I would say to you, unable to concentrate because of my poor health, I picked up the *Divine Comedy* and for the first time, precisely because of the subject which I had on my mind: that spiritual fatherhood of which we are speaking, I found the leading theme in that difficult work of the great poet. I urge you to read Dante in order to guide your novices through hell and purgatory, and up to heaven, because in the *Divine Comedy* he skillfully describes a spiritual journey, and the spiritual masters of Dante—Virgil, Beatrice, Saint Bernard—have one trait in common: their smile! They smile all the time, and it is often enough for them to smile in order to be understood and followed by their disciple. . . . In the *Divine Comedy,* that poetical summa of the Middle Ages, there is (thus) an allusion to the doctrine of Saint Bernard on the image. And that which touches Dante and moves him is the PERFECT REPRODUCTION OF BERNARD'S INTERIOR CHARITY AND PEACE ON HIS FEATURES, in his smile and his

15. Br. Patrick Ryan, ocso, "Friendship and Sublety," *Monastic Exchange* 8, 2 (Summer, 1976) 17–19.

whole bearing, just as the features of Jesus left an imprint on the image of the true God on Veronica's veil.

I have found three characteristic traits of the relation between Dante and his spiritual guides: First, Dante shows himself a DOCILE DISCIPLE, frequently comparing his feelings to those of a child who is astonished, surprised, and dependent on his masters . . . Secondly, the RELATION BETWEEN MASTER AND DISCIPLE IS EXTREMELY QUICK, DELICATE, AND UNDERSTANDING, interpersonal, as we would say today . . . Finally, the third important note: THE GOAL OF SPIRITUAL GUIDANCE IS TO MAKE A PERSON FREE, TO HELP HIM GRADUALLY BECOME CAPABLE OF TAKING CARE OF HIMSELF . . . And Saint Bernard, after having told Dante to look at the face which comes closest to that of Christ and of God, namely Mary's because only her light can prepare him to see Christ, encourages him to make the last stage of his journey alone.[16]

The 1974 Laval seminar was followed in October by an intensive two-week workshop at Chimay, entitled simply *Quinzaine cistercienne* and structured on the theme: *The monastic perception of the twelfth-Century Cistercians*. The abbesses had been so pleased with the results of the 1972 Patristic-Cistercian Trimester that they had asked the secretaries for formation for more of the same. As its title implied, this shorter course was entirely centered on the Cistercian Fathers. The lecturers were Fr. Maur, Fr. Charles, Fr. Corneille Halflants and Br. Gabriel from Scourmont, and also Fr. Edmond Mikkers and Fr. André Fracheboud. A second trimester was already being planned for autumn, 1975.

The nuns' Quinzaine had scarcely finished when Fr. Maur and Fr. Charles had to start thinking about the Law Commission meeting scheduled for the middle of November, 1974, at Scourmont. The main subject on the agenda was the Constitutions, so that the meeting risked lasting longer than usual, perhaps even for a month! Fr. Charles wrote to a friend, "I am unwell and unfit

16. C. Dumont, "Dante revisited." Trans. Patrick Ryan, ocso, *Monastic Exchange* 8, 3 (Fall, 1976) 70–72.

for work. A one-month-long meeting! That would finish me!" (10.24.74). As it happened, early in November he became quite ill and had to be hospitalized at Saint Pierre Clinic in Louvain. A few days later Dom Guerric, on his way to the airport to pick up a member of the Law Commission, stopped at the hospital to see how his sick monk was getting along. Fortunately, he was improving and could soon return to Scourmont, just in time to attend the last sessions of the Law Commission meeting.

This most recent bout with illness obliged Fr. Charles to cancel his trip to Gethsemani for the seminar planned for early 1975. The seminar did take place, but with a somewhat different orientation than originally planned. Nevertheless, the guidelines he had drawn up remained valid and in his future teaching he followed them.

Father Charles' teaching

What exactly had Fr. Charles been teaching in Europe and North America during these last several years? Summarily, his lectures could be classified under three titles: Cistercian Monastic life, Saint Bernard, Saint Aelred. Some of the principal topics were:

- why we should read our Cistercian Fathers;
- the Cistercians' trans-historical value;
- the balance to maintain among the three principal aspects of the Benedictine/Cistercian life: prayer, *lectio,* work;
- the Cistercian tradition as a school of charity;
- spiritual friendship;
- devotion to the Humanity of Christ.

One conference was entitled *Finding a formula in a time of renewal*. The retreats he gave during this period—and they were numerous—were centered on Cistercian simplicity, the all-embracing foundation of the Cistercian way of life. Some of the most important texts from Saint Bernard's works which Fr. Charles chose to comment upon were *Sermon 20 on the Song of Songs,* on why God took on human form; his principal treatises: *On Humility, On Loving God, On Grace and Free Will, On Consideration, On Conversion* and *Sermons 80–82 On the Song of Songs* on the image of God. This last theme was studied also in Aelred's *Mirror of Charity,* as were also the faculty of love and spiritual friendship. The importance of conforming one's will to God's will, of consenting to grace, came up over and over again in these various contexts. All the texts were chosen in view of assisting the monk or nun to seek God truly and love Him more deeply. Besides speaking about the early Cistercians, he tended to make digressions and comment on questions which were being debated currently in the Order.

The response to his talks in both Europe and North America touched him deeply. From an American monastery he had written: "The receptivity to Cistercian spirituality is surprising, and very consoling for someone who is 'proclaiming the good news to the ends of the world' (cf. Ps 18:5) . . . . I am convinced that a renewal: *novum monasterium-schola caritatis rediviva* could come to light (i.e., after this period of change) in this country. Everywhere there is youthful eagerness to actualize the tradition" (3.23.74).

It should be remembered that what one might call devotional spirituality characterized many communities in the pre-1960 years. Few texts of the Cistercian Fathers were available in English in those days, and when Saint Bernard *was* quoted the passages were usually limited to edifying phrases or paragraphs. In many—probably most—monasteries the monastic theology spoken of by Dom Jean Leclercq had not yet been assimilated, so that when Fr. Charles arrived with a rich theological presentation of the Fathers for many monks and nuns it was an exhilarating first, like something they had been waiting for without knowing exactly what. The reaction was often the same as it had been for the nuns at the first Trimester when they said: "*Ça colle à la vie,*" that is to say, "This goes with our life!" During the next years—from 1975 until the early 1980s—Fr. Charles presented this same teaching in various ways in monasteries in Europe, especially in houses of nuns. Because of persisting poor health, however, he did not return to North America again until 1991.

As has been pointed out, Fr. Charles' lectures on the Fathers were often enhanced by quotations from poets, dramatists or philosophers. These added the aesthetic character which he insisted upon as being essential in the Cistercian life. One loves what is beautiful, and what is more beautiful than God's Truth and Love . . . or a human will in total agreement with God's will? The aesthetic side of the Cistercians' teaching is also akin to simplicity. In his talk on *The monk in the Church* at Mortefontaine, near Paris, Fr. Charles said: "Liturgy is not one of my strong points, but simplicity seems to me to be a condition required for the spontaneity which we would like to rediscover. The serenity of faith is a charism."[17]

It was fortunate that Fr. Charles had withdrawn from the project for the Gethsemani Workshop because at the time it took place he was still feeling very weak after his recent hospitalization. He was feeling so unwell, in fact, that he gave over the editorship of *Collectanea* to Brother Gabriel, although he himself remained associate editor. In the hope of restoring his health he went south again to the Monastery of the Paix-Dieu. Visits to Cabanoule did him good. He enjoyed the lifestyle and atmosphere in this new, small foundation, as well as the sisters' interest in his talks. It was during this visit to the Paix–Dieu in 1975 that, on the feast of Our Lord's Presentation in the Temple, he had the moving experience of baptizing Brother Paul, an elderly hermit who lived in a trailer-like cabin perched on a hillside off the winding road leading up to the monastery. Brother Paul was a colorful personality. He had been an Anglican Cowley religious for fifteen years in Boston, then later on had turned to a solitary life. The ecumenically-oriented nuns of the Paix-Dieu had more or less adopted him. On previous visits Fr. Charles had occasions to visit Brother Paul and enjoyed talking to him. This time, when Fr. Charles arrived in January, Brother Paul told him that he had

17. "Une communauté dans l'Eglise," *Collectanea* 34 (1972) 293. Trans. "A Community in the Church," *Cistercian Studies* VIII (1973) 273–289.

been waiting for him so that he could become a Catholic! His baptism was a joy for the whole community.

In April Fr. Charles was again at Caldey. As always, he had several volumes of Saint Bernard's works within easy reach. While reading Sermon 87 *De Diversis* he lingered over the following phrase which is one of the rare literal patristic quotations found in Saint Bernard's works : "Contemplation is the fruit of the Word of God's merciful descent to our human nature by grace, which elevates human nature to the Word Himself by love of God." Fr. Charles took pleasure in tracing this phrase back to its origin: from Bernard to Scotus Eriugena to Maximos the Confessor to Gregory of Nazianzen, and finally to Origen. Several years later, in a lecture at a formation meeting he commented on this quotation: "It is the whole Eastern tradition that Saint Bernard was summarizing here when he called human salvation the *divine philanthropy* which descends to his human creature. Saint Bernard speaks of the celestial man who became a terrestrial man, who came down to earth so that *theophilia* might occur, that is to say, that man might ascend to God by loving Him."[18]

From Caldey Fr. Charles returned to France, where he gave retreats at Port-du-Salut and Laval. Back at Scourmont for the summer his health was much better; fortunately, because July and August were months of intense activity. He had an article to write on *Saint Bernard et les Cisterciens* for the *Grande Encyclopédie Larousse* and was up to his neck in articles and reviews for the *Bulletin.* He was also invited to participate in a meeting at Scourmont concerning *Pain de Cîteaux,* but after the first hour of discussion was obliged to withdraw to his room to rest. There he wrote a poem on Mary Magdalen, whose feast day it was. He had recently moved into a new room at Scourmont. From his window he could see a beautiful birch tree which became the subject of another of his poems.[19]

18. *Chapitre 7 de la Règle de saint Benoît*. Workshop for Novice Directors of Western France, Bayeux, 1979. "Le cinquième degré d'humilité; l'ouverture de coeur et le sacrement de pénitence," 84–109. Reprinted in *Sagesse ardente,* 195–212. See 196–197, with notes 1–4.

19. "L'arbre," *Poèmes et Prières,* 27.

A little later he spent a few days at the monastery of Soleilmont, giving several lectures to the sisters on the principal characteristics of Cistercian spirituality: simplicity, authenticity, truth . . .

The second Trimester

The most important occupation Fr. Charles had before him toward the end of the summer was preparation of his lectures for the second Chimay trimester which would begin in October. The theme this time was *The Holy Spirit.* As in 1972, Fr. Maur had put together an impressive program with some equally impressive lecturers. As in 1972, the three Scourmont monks: Fr. Maur, Fr. Charles and Br. Gabriel were available to advise and guide the students in their personal study projects. Generally speaking, the nuns at this trimester were younger than the participants at the first trimester, among whom there had been several novice mistresses and prioresses. Another difference from the first trimester was that lectures were frequently scheduled in the afternoon as well as in the morning, which changed the rhythm of the monastic day somewhat. When the sisters returned to their monasteries in December it was with a deepened understanding of the Cistercian life and a desire to continue their studies at home.

Fr. Charles' agenda was full of retreats and lectures scheduled for the first three months of 1976. Besides these, Dom André Louf, president of the Central Europe Regional Conference, had invited him to give a talk at the regional meeting to be held at Cîteaux in June. The topic suggested to him was: *Cîteaux in our Times and the Sensitivity of Young People,* but he was reticent about using the term "young people" because it seemed to suggest a sort of class distinction, and proposed instead: *The Spirit of Cîteaux in Our Times.* His talk on communion with the Founders of Cîteaux in the contemporary setting was interspersed with quotations ranging from Saint Bernard and the *Exordium Parvum* to T.S. Eliot and Olivier Clément, from whom he drew insights applicable to the Cistercian charism. He also touched upon the subject of the form of the Cistercian life, which the Fathers modestly but significantly called *formula institutionis nostrae.* Concretely, this formula comes down to two basic attitudes, simplicity and authenticity, which the first Cistercians understood in the following way and which Fr. Charles stressed constantly in his teaching:

> The essential characteristic of their (the Cistercians') initiative surfaces as simplicity in their life style, and rejection of everything that appeared to them to be without purpose and superfluous . . . This simplicity is a fundamental attitude, a spiritual instinct which must be acquired. It manifested itself at Cîteaux by rejection of whatever was superfluous, sham or artificial. Our Fathers thought that artificiality had been introduced by compromise with the world and the social and political obligations that sprang from feudalism . . . We do not need to mention here how simplicity was manifested in Cistercian art. Authenticity, which is truly characteristic of Cîteaux, means being grounded in the truth, being subject to the nature of things. . . . How can a person become simple? By living in contact with reality each day. . . . The spirit of simplicity requires persistent and progressive ascesis.[20]

In this same lecture Fr. Charles also touched upon subjects which he often developed when he spoke to communities: experience, tradition, interior life, the aesthetic character of monastic life and studies for monks and nuns.

The fourth Seminar for Novice Mistresses, on the theme *Personalism and Community,* took place at Laval from September 16 to 24. Fr. Charles had been asked to present Aelred's teaching in this context.[21] In October and November he gave lectures in several monasteries in the north of France and in Belgium, including Orval, where he spent a week studying Saint Bernard with the novices and juniors. The next year he was once more scheduled for extended lecture tours in France, Belgium and Switzerland:

20. "The Spirit of Cîteaux in Our Times," *Monastic Exchange* 9. 1 (Spring, 1977) 16–17.

21. See "Personalism in Community according to Aelred of Rievaulx," *Cistercian Studies* XII (1977) 250–271.

one in January and February, another in the summer, and the last from September until November, before returning home to Scourmont for Advent and Christmas.

Once again, Constitutions

At the meeting of the Consilium Generale in October, 1976, several votes were taken concerning work to be entrusted to the Law Commission. Briefly, the Abbots wanted some samples of what the future Constitutions could perhaps be like, so that they could study them at the 1977 General Chapter. They also wanted the Law Commission to draw up a new Statute for itself. So from the 7th until the 11th of December Fr. Charles was busy at a Law Commission meeting. It was his last. The 1977 General Chapter approved a new Statute for the Commission and elected new members, with Dom Bernard Johnson as President. Some time later, in a talk to the sisters at Soleilmont, when reminiscing about his years as a member of the Commission he said that he had been the theologian for the Law Commission, but that every time he raised his weak voice it was immediately snuffed out by the roar of canons.

Although migraine headaches recurred at frequent intervals and left Fr. Charles prostrate, after these bouts he often snapped back with extraordinary resilience and felt very well, such as happened at Easter that year. Often after being ill he would have new inspirations or insights, as though the migraine had been a catalyst! Still, sometimes in the evening before leaving on a lecture trip he would find himself anxious about whether he would be in shape for travelling the next morning.

For this monk-poet who was "always thinking of something else," traveling could indeed be trying. On one trip to Cabanoule after Christmas, at the *Gare de Lyon* he found himself caught up in a crowd of Parisian students off to Savoy to ski during the holidays. The only vacant place he could find in the train was at the end of a car where there were two seats reserved for disabled war veterans *(mutilés de guerre)*. He had other adventures, but when he found himself in real difficulty there always seemed to be some kind soul around who would offer to help him.

In Switzerland

In September Fr. Charles conducted retreats at the Fille-Dieu and the Maigrauge, as well as at the monasteries of the Bernardine nuns at Collombey and Géronde. While he was with the Bernardines he became very interested in the writings and reform of their foundress, Louyse de Ballon, a young seventeenth-century nun whose vision was so closely in keeping with the goals of the early Cistercians. He was in fact so impressed by this courageous young nun's teaching and its value for contemporary monastics that he wrote an article on her for *Collectanea*.[22] The keynote of Mother de Ballon's reform was simplicity. This is not surprising, since she had modeled her teaching on Saint Bernard's:

> The simplicity which is the predominant note of her whole spirituality has none of the aesthetic elegance that can be admired in modesty and reserve. For her, simplicity meant the cross of Christ and the narrow door of renunciation and sacrifice. Uniting these two considerations, she said of her reform that the passion of the Saviour was its principal founder, and that the religious were to have it unceasingly before their eyes . . . Simplicity desires nothing but God.[23]

The monastery of Géronde is situated near Sierre, in the part of Valais where the great poet Rainer Maria Rilke (whom Fr. Charles preferred perhaps above all other poets) had lived the last

22. "La simplicité comme principe de réforme chez la Mère Louyse de Ballon," *Collectanea* 41 (1979) 73–93. Trans. "Simplicity as a principle of Reform in the writings of Mère Louyse de Ballon," *Hidden Springs. Cistercian religious women*, volume III, Book 2 (Kalamazoo: Cistercian Publications, 1995) 575–597.

23. Ibid., 581.

years of his life. Fr. Charles had the joy of visiting the Château of Muzot, Rilke's last residence where he completed the *Duino Elegies,* as well as the graveyard at Raron where the poet was buried. His visit to Valais coincided with the gathering of the grapes in the region's rich vineyards. The towering mountains, the mellow touch of September sunlight, the fragrance of the earth and vines, all contributed to making his sojourn memorable. Before leaving Géronde, he wrote a poem:

Valais

Poids des rochers
Elan des cîmes
Foi des clochers
Frôlant l'abîme

Grises montagnes
Sans compromis
Vertes campagnes
Aux fruits promis

Fleuve du temps
Fluide et stable
Présent chantant
Vins sur la table.

La vie est là
Douce et extrême
Et sans éclat
Comme je l'aime.

Valais

Weight of rocks
Summits' upward thrust
Bell towers' faith
Lightly skimming the abyss.

Gray mountains
Uncompromising
Green countrysides
Promising fruit.

River of time
Flowing and stable
Singing the present moment
Wines on the table.

Life is there
Sweet and extreme
And without glitter
As I like it.[24]

Several years later Fr. Charles returned to Géronde for lectures. From the window of his room he had a splendid view: "'I lift my eyes to the mountains,' like the Psalmist. They are very beautiful here, with a little snow on the summits." After accompanying the nuns' chaplain to an exposition on Rilke, he wrote: "There was a lady with us who is the daughter of the man who tolled the bell during Rilke's funeral, and that was what I found most moving."

24. *Prières et Poèmes,* 55.

More Retreats and Lectures

Although Fr. Charles had not been able to attend the workshop for formation personnel in the United States, he did participate in several such projects in France. First of all, there were two more Seminars for Novice Mistresses at Laval: on *Formation* (1979) and on the *The twelfth-century Cistercians' re-reading of the Rule* (1982).[25] His contributions at both these seminars were of primary importance. We might say that the three talks he gave on formation could be a handbook for formators of novices and juniors. The first lecture dealt with *The origin of the form of the Cistercian life,* the second: *Transmission of the form of the Cistercian life,* and the third: *Transformation by conformation to Christ*. As always, everything Fr. Charles said pointed toward following Christ in every aspect of the Cistercian life and growing in love of God by progressively bringing one's will into accordance with God's will.

It was in 1978 that Fr. Charles for the first time received an invitation to be the resource person at a meeting of the Cistercian and Benedictine novice masters and mistresses of the west of France, a number of whom he already knew. Fr. Charles met with this group three consecutive years, to reflect on Chapter VII of the Rule: on the third step of humility in 1978, on the fifth in 1979 and on the twelfth in 1980.

It was also in 1978 that Fr. Charles was appointed non-resident chaplain for the nuns of Soleilmont. Msgr. Himmer, the retired bishop of Tournai who had ordained Fr. Charles, resided at Soleilmont, so the nuns were assured of daily Mass. For his ministry as chaplain Fr. Charles usually spent three days there every fortnight. He remained chaplain at Soleilmont for twenty-two years. When he celebrated his Golden Jubilee of ordination to the priesthood on May 18, 2000, it was at Soleilmont that he

25. Fr. Charles' talks at both these seminars were published first in a booklet *hors commerce* printed at Laval Abbey. Several of them were reprinted in *Sagesse ardente* (Oka: Abbaye Notre-Dame du Lac, 1995) *Pain de Cîteaux* 8, 3rd series. See Ch. 6. "La relecture de la Règle de saint Benoît par les Cisterciens du XIIe siècle" 101–138 and Ch. 12, a revised version of "La formation cistercienne," 263–326.

chose to celebrate the Eucharist that day because it was there, he said, that he had exercised his priestly ministry most.

In September, 1978, Fr. Charles attended the South/West France Regional Meeting, to which he had been invited primarily to comment on the study made for the Law Commission on the question of nuns' chaplains. Unfortunately, his remarks were inaccurately recorded in the Minutes of the meeting and this bothered him.

Saint Michel College and Fontevrault

In the course of the next two years two special engagements found place on Fr. Charles' agenda, fitted in among his lectures in monasteries. Firstly, he was invited by the Jesuits of the Institute for Theological Studies at Saint Michel College in Brussels to give a lecture on the theology of Saint Bernard. The "old boy" of Saint Michel felt honored and pleased to return to his alma mater after so many years, speaking to Jesuits and their theology students as a Cistercian monk! He found the audience very stimulating and thoroughly enjoyed that visit.

The other speaking engagement was at the Fontevrault Cultural Center in France in the context of a celebration for the fifteenth centennial of Saint Benedict's birth. In the magnificently restored abbey founded by Robert d'Arbrissel and governed in the Middle Ages by abbesses aided in administration by men, Fr. Charles began his talk by telling his distinguished audience that he was not a historian, but rather a historian of spirituality, and that any historical allusions which might come up in his talk would be due to the fact that he was in the presence of the *gisants* of Henri II Plantagenêt and Aliénor of Aquitaine, Fontevrault's patroness. From there, he went on to speak about Abélard and Saint Bernard. Here it is not possible even to summarize this unpublished paper, but Fr. Charles brought out that one of the aspects of the conflict between these two men was the vision each had of the Church. Saint Bernard was clearly opposed to Abélard's ambitious idea and desire that monks should be at the center or summit of the Church as dialecticians or learned theologians. The Abbot of Clairvaux had the firm but humble conviction that monks are brought together as Christians, and that their communal and personal prayer unites them with all human beings. Fr. Charles commented:

> When we reflect on the lives of these two men, and their sincerity—which, I believe, was authentic in each case—we should not judge them. Nor should we judge the history or the daily life of either one, but if we want to try to estimate (as Abélard would, we might say) what was important for each one, we would have to say that as Saint Bernard saw it the integration of human and Christian values, and consequently monastic values, was much greater. What saved Bernard, in comparison to Abélard who finally was unhappy with his utopian ideal, was that Saint Bernard had a firm conception of the Church as an institution as well as its being the Mystical Body. That was because in his theology and spirituality the Incarnation played the central role. All of Saint Bernard's spirituality, all of his mystical theology has as its central point *the Word made flesh* so that man may reach God. There is a reciprocal movement: the humility of God, who comes to share our human condition and experience it. . . .
>
> For Saint Bernard the Church is a divine milieu, not that he identifies it solely as the visible Church, but because the invisible Church is indissolubly bound to the visible Church just as the Word was united to the visible Body of Christ. For Saint Bernard that is absolutely indispensable for salvation. When we speak of the Church today, whether as an institution or as the Mystical Body, we perhaps do not possess the same realism as Saint Bernard and his monks did. For them the monastic community was a realization of the microcosm, the *ecclesiola* (as Bernard says: "the little church"), the Church lived in the context of human fraternal relationships, both difficult and enriching, and also in relationships of friendship. When I read the life of Abélard, I was struck by the fact that he didn't have any friends: he was all alone. That was heroic, but it certainly did not help

> him. Saint Bernard always had friends; he was always surrounded by friendly people. Community life also gave him support. Like a guide, it contributed to helping him to be faithful to his interior orientation.[26]

During the second half of 1980, Fr. Charles remained at Scourmont most of the time. There were always reviews to be prepared for *Collectanea,* and in August he was scheduled to give a series of lectures on Saint Bernard at Scourmont for twenty Bernardine nuns of the Audenarde Congregation. He was also finishing up an Introduction to the Spanish edition of Saint Bernard's works and editing the lectures he had given in France to the Benedictine and Cistercian novice directors. "A huge job," he sighed with relief when he had put the final touches on it. Two hundred copies of this 190-page mimeographed booklet on *Chapter 7 of the Rule* were quickly snapped up, so that a second printing was necessary.

In December Fr. Charles left for Acey to give the annual retreat, the only time he ever accepted a retreat right before Christmas. In fact, it ended on Christmas Eve so that it was with the monks of Acey, in their twelfth century church, that he celebrated the feast of the Lord's Nativity. He then went to Switzerland to preach retreats at La Maigrauge, La Fille-Dieu and Collombey. After his return to Scourmont he wrote to a friend:

> My health is not satisfactory . . . Pray for me, that I may be in better shape or just go to heaven, but perhaps the two are contradictory, and I must suffer to enter the kingdom. I am contented although unsatisfied . . . I have finally understood that the two are compatible! (4.5.81)

Between May and September, 1981, Fr. Charles was hospitalized four times at Saint Luke Hospital in Brussels. There he underwent two operations, one in July and the other toward the end of September. When this ordeal was finally over, after several weeks of convalescence at Soleilmont he was able to return to

26. "Abélard contre Saint Bernard." Unpublished lecture. (Fontevrault: October, 1979) 5.

Scourmont. That year the weather was milder than usual, and from the window of his room he had a "peaceful and luminous view. What more do we need to be happy—*humano modo*—interim?" (11.25.81) he mused.

Fr. Charles kept busy with multiple tasks, including a course on the *Mirror of Charity* he was giving in the novitiate and his translation of the *Mirror* which he had been working on off and on for several years. As he looked over the text he kept making new discoveries. The following is a good example of how he worked:

> All the last part of Aelred's sermon for Palm Sunday . . . is remarkable and a true commentary on the *Speculum,* because even the word *speculum* occurs with its meaning. My work on the *Speculum* will be useful for the lecture I am supposed to give at the Laval Seminar in September, 1982, on *Re-reading of the Rule by the twelfth-century Cistercians*. (11.25.81)

The passage from the Palm Sunday sermon to which he was referring reads as follows:

> I am speaking to you, my brothers, my sons, you who are not only adorers of Christ's cross but who profess this cross. You not only profess this cross, but are lovers of it. I am speaking to you, and each one can think as he wishes, judge as he wishes, forge illusions as much as he wants: in Christ's cross there is nothing tender, nothing soft, nothing delicate, nothing pleasant for the flesh and blood (cf. Spec II.9). So let this cross be henceforth like a mirror for the Christian. Let him look at himself in the cross of Christ to see if his own life and his way of living is in agreement with this cross. To the extent that he participates in the cross of Christ, he can hope to share in Christ's glory (cf. 2 Tm 2:1-12) . . . You, my brothers, see how you should rejoice, you who are crucified with Christ himself.[27]

With the return of spring, 1982, Fr. Charles set out for Landévennec, in France, where he was to be the resource person at

27. Aelred of Rievaulx, *Sermon for Palm Sunday 29. Sermo In Ramis Palmorum* X.29. Corpus Christianorum Continuatio Medievaelis IIA, 87–88.

another meeting of Cistercian and Benedictine formation directors. The theme this time was prayer. Two of Fr. Charles' talks were based on Msgr. Nédoncelle's fine book: *Prière humaine, prière divine,*[28] in which the author referred to Aelred of Rievaulx's method of meditation. In September of that year, the sixth seminar for Cistercian novice mistresses was held at Laval. Then, on October 9, at the request of his friend, Bishop Jean Huard, Fr. Charles began a series of five Saturday morning talks on *The Spirituality of Saint Bernard* at the seminary at Tournai. Because the Abbot of Clairvaux's teaching is so Christocentric, Fr. Charles developed at length his teaching on the Incarnation. Although principally for seminarians, these lectures were also open to the public. During the winter of 1982–1983 Fr. Charles continued to go to Soleilmont regularly for confessions and a talk or two to the community, and from time to time went for ministry to La Paix in Chimay or to the Bernardine nuns in Charleville, but otherwise his activity was limited by a recurrence of his illness. On April 13 he underwent surgery at Saint Luke Hospital. Before long, however, it became evident that this last operation had not had the desired result. The two specialists who had been treating him decided that a radical operation was necessary. So it was that in the middle of August he was operated on for a definitive ablation of the ileum.

When this eight-hour operation was all over and he was coming to the first thing he heard was a nurse's voice urging him to "Breathe! Breathe!" After having successfully gone through this extreme ordeal, the doctors did not want to lose Fr. Charles simply because it didn't occur to him to breathe! But let the patient tell his story:

> After the operation, while I was still under the effects of the anaesthesia I felt so happy that I refused to make the effort that the nurse was asking of me, that is, to breathe! Finally she said: "If you don't breathe, you are going to die" . . . I was praying to the Blessed Virgin, with the Hail

28. M. Nédoncelle, *Prière humaine, prière divine* (Paris: Desclée de Brouwer, 1962).

> Mary in Greek!: *χαιρε κεχαριτωμενη*. I hadn't recited it in the original for more than twenty years. But there was the word "fruit"—*καρπος*—that I couldn't think of. And when I decided to breathe and to live, to the surprise of the nurse and doctor I cried out triumphantly: *καρπος*!, which I had to explain. I believe that the Blessed Virgin was somehow present (Sept. '83).[29]

The day after the operation, before going to Brussels to see Fr. Charles Dom Guerric stopped off at Notre-Dame de la Paix for a few minutes. On the spur of the moment Olga, a sister from Soleilmont who was portress at Chimay at that time, went out into the guesthouse garden and gathered a bouquet of roses in full bloom which she gave to Dom Guerric for his suffering monk. Later, when Fr. Charles spoke of the days immediately following his operation, he said that all he was able to do was to let his gaze rest on those roses. His days in intensive care were a period of total weakness and dependence, but also of interiority. He was reduced to zero and didn't even know if he was still alive! For several days he was unable to think or pray. One single thing remained, something that he could not really express in words: an interior perception of the Body of Christ, a communication in the Spirit . . . the Church. These thoughts were like blood flowing through his veins. Later, when speaking about the poetic life being communication in the Spirit, as in the Body of Christ, the Church, he referred to this experience which he felt had been a very important time of grace for him. At the end of August he was able to leave the hospital walking on his own two feet. Normally he would not have been released so soon, but the doctors knew that at Soleilmont where he was going for his convalescence he would have the nuns' attentive care and especially that of Sr. Agnes, an excellent nurse.

29. More than ten years later, Fr. Charles saw a letter in *The Tablet* by a British lady who had had an analogous experience during which she felt the Blessed Virgin's presence. Fr. Charles wrote to her and they compared notes, so to speak.

Finally, as the autumn foliage was beginning to turn red, copper and gold, on October 6 he returned to Scourmont. It took him a long time to regain his strength. To avoid the winter dampness and chill, he spent part of December and January in the south of France, at Castagniers and Cabanoule, drawing encouragement from the warmth of the sun and the nuns' interest in the Cistercian Fathers. He was well enough to give the annual retreat in each of these monasteries, and in early February gave several talks at Laval on the philosophy of Gabriel Marcel and Pope John Paul II's theatre-piece: *Brother of our God.* Toward the end of February, 1984, he resumed his ministry as chaplain at Soleilmont.

Once Fr. Charles had recovered from this great trial, he resumed his other activities, but less intensively than before. There were fewer lectures. His articles continued to appear in *Collectanea* and to be translated into Spanish and English. It has been mentioned that new inspirations seemed to come to Fr. Charles after his terrible migraines. After the life-threatening ordeal he had been through everything he wrote seemed to be marked by new profundity and beauty.

5

IN THE SCHOOL OF CHARITY WITH BERNARD AND AELRED

Believe me, the Cistercian Fathers present a summit of spiritual achievement perhaps never reached before or since.

C. D.

Fr. Charles' convalescence after his serious operation in 1983 took a long time. Nevertheless, he continued writing and teaching. His first article to appear in *Collectanea* during this period was *Lire Saint Bernard aujourd'hui* which reflects very well the existential and humanist character of his reflection. The principal thrust is that people in our post-modern world find themselves confronted with the same basic questions of human existence as in the past. "It would not be a waste of time to re-read the teaching of Saint Bernard on captive liberty, on simplicity that (in a technocratic society) has become duplicity, on mortal immortality, on self-will and obedience, and on all the themes related to the image of God present in man but shattered. The Christian lives in two worlds. He cannot content himself with living in one to the exclusion of the other."[1] His approach was that of a philosopher and poet. From this time until the end of the decade, only

1. "Lire Saint Bernard aujourd'hui," *Collectanea* 46 (1984) 272–290. Trans. "Reading Saint Bernard Today," *Cistercian Studies* XXII (1987) 152–171. Here, 162.

two more articles signed by him appeared in *Collectanea:* one on Thomas Merton and one on Aelred.[2]

In the Order, the torrents of change and turmoil had been forded, generally speaking. The Abbots and Abbesses were advancing toward finalizing their Constitutions. This meant that a certain level of stability had been reached which permitted more concentration on Cistercian spirituality and its implications for life in the monasteries. Fr. Charles had two principal preoccupations at this time. The first was to finish the translation of Aelred's *Mirror of Charity*. The second was to write a work on Saint Bernard's spiritual theology; he had been meditating on this for a long time. During the second half of the 1980s almost all his lectures were related to Aelred's *Mirror of Charity* or to Saint Bernard's works. He received many invitations to give series of talks, especially to communities of nuns in France and Switzerland. Some of these monasteries he visited each year, so that he got to know many of the sisters personally. Their interest and questions when he spoke of the diverse aspects of Saint Bernard's teaching stimulated his own reflection. It was also during this period (in November, 1985) that the formators of the Italian communities invited Fr. Charles to be the resource person at their meeting at Tre Fontane. The topic chosen was Cistercian anthropology, which went hand in hand with his plan for a synthesis on Saint Bernard. In addition to all that, Fr. Charles was also giving a course to the novices at Scourmont. To him it was all the same if he gave a course to two people or to fifty because, as he said, the one who profits most is always the professor.

One day a reporter from Radio Notre-Dame came to Scourmont to interview Fr. Charles about the Cistercian Fathers and Thomas Merton. After listening to Fr. Charles' answers to his questions the interviewer remarked that the way he talked about

2. "La vocation de Thomas Merton," *Collectanea* 48 (1986) 9–18. Trans. "The Vocation of Thomas Merton," *Cistercian Studies* XXIII (1988) 242–253, and "L'amour fraternel dans la doctrine monastique d'Aelred de Rievaulx," *Collectanea* 51 (1989) 79–88. "Fraternal Love in the Monastic Doctrine of Aelred of Rievaulx," Trans. Patricia Carroll, ocso, *Cistercian Studies Quarterly* XXXII (1997) 25–35.

the Fathers astonished him; it was as though they were his friends. This of course pleased Fr. Charles, because by his continual study of the writings of Saint Bernard and Saint Aelred they had actually become his close friends, just as Merton had. This came through in his teaching, too, and gave it a very living character.

With his thoughts dwelling on his work at hand, he wrote:

> When I prepared my course on Saint Bernard's anthropology, after re-reading the *Sermons on the Song of Songs* I came to the conclusion that we must begin with the vision of God and the human being made in his image. If we begin with the human being, we do not find the ancient approach. Actually, we must begin with Christ, then his spouse, the Church, then the communion of saints, and finally, the human being. (3.16.86)

For him, Saint Bernard's *Sermons on the Song of Songs* were the key to the whole Cistercian genius, and he would have liked to have seen the General Chapter take more interest in the Cistercian Fathers' teaching.

Even if Fr. Charles was at last freed of his most important health problem, he continued to be plagued by other ills. The next year he underwent two operations: one in July for kidney stones and the other, in October, for prostate problems. Between the two operations he went to Caldey to rest. Like most monasteries, Caldey had changed considerably during the post-Vatican II period. Perched high on a cliff one day, he thought back over the years when he taught the juniors on Caldey Island, and wrote: "Here I find nothing of the life I knew in the '50s. Only the sea and the rocks are the same. Since then, generations of seagulls have come and gone. And what remains of the young monk of those days? Maybe a little of this desire for the absolute and eternity which I sometimes go to find at the edge of the waves" (5.26.86).

When Father Charles got back to Scourmont he learned that the book *Prières aux quatre temps* had just come off the press.[3]

3. *Prières aux quatre temps. Des poèmes et des chants* (Paris: Centurion, 1986) 180–198.

Only very rarely did Fr. Charles write texts for the liturgy—that was not his style exactly—but this volume of liturgical poems and hymns included some of his work. Among the books he was reading at that time was Martin Buber's: *I and Thou* and some essays which followed this remarkable work written in the 1920s. In his notes he wrote:

> When reading this book today, one realizes how far we have gone since then in the anonymous way of collectivism. Even in the monasteries we cannot escape this atmosphere where no one really meets anyone else and where there is no real presence. He (Buber) is very close to Gabriel Marcel, and I can understand why he has been criticized for copying him, although this is not true. The danger of an illusory community is very real. But in no matter what situation we find ourselves we can save our soul, and in the last analysis circumstances have so little influence on our real life. (12.22.86)

Changing the subject, he added: "I don't know where we are with renewal. I believe that personal spiritual life is not given its proper value, and it is the essential thing without which everything else is insignificant."

The winter of 1987 was very severe in Europe. Fr. Charles stayed in his room most of the time, venturing out only for the Eucharistic concelebration each day. Though his spirits were sometimes low he remained patiently tranquil, waiting for God's grace: *Tranquillus Deus tranquillat omnia.*[4] As Holy Week approached, he expressed in a few words the substance of his meditation: "May the Mystery of the Cross give us the joy of salvation and limitless hope" (3.16.87). The Cross, joy, salvation, hope. Everything is there.

Shortly before Pentecost Fr. Charles ventured as far as Laval, where he spoke to the sisters about his recent commentary on Saint Bernard's *Treatise on Precept and Dispensation.* Afterwards, both surprised and happy, he told a friend: "The day before my last lectures I made a synthesis of Saint Bernard's spirituality in

4. Bernard of Clairvaux, SC 23.16. *Sancti Bernardi Opera* 1:149.

forty-five minutes! I astonished myself, and was really pleased! As Dom Anselme Le Bail used to say, 'Thirty years of study for one hour of synthesis'" (Pentecost, 1987). When summer came he visited several other monasteries in the south of France, speaking either on Aelred (having in mind the Introduction to the *Mirror of Charity* which he was working on) or Saint Bernard's *Treatise on Grace and Free Choice.* At the same time he was reading Claudel's commentaries on Scripture, where he was happy to find in beautiful French the same spiritual sense as in Saint Bernard. In *Le Vocabulaire philosophique de Gabriel Marcel* he found a phrase that remained with him: "To be is to resist in the trial of life."[5] This thought coincided well with his own intuitions and came up in his later writings as being fundamental.

Meanwhile, for the first time in history, the General Chapters of both Abbots and Abbesses, concurrent with a Mixed General Meeting, took place in Rome. After twenty years of work new *Constitutions* were voted upon by each Chapter. This was Dom Guerric's last Chapter. After a long tenure as superior, first as Apostolic Administrator during Dom Anselme Le Bail's illness, and then as Abbot since 1956, he had reached seventy-five years of age in August, 1988, and in keeping with the Constitutions offered his resignation. Dom Guerric was succeeded by Dom Thomas Vilain, who was elected in October and received the abbatial blessing on December 8.

The French translation of the *Speculum caritatis,* preceded by a short introduction, was finished. Fr. Charles asked Sr. Gaëtane de Briey, of Clairefontaine, to go over his manuscript and then sent it to Bellefontaine Editions where it was to be published in their *Vie Monastique* series.[6]

5. Gabriel Marcel, *Journal Métaphysique* (Paris: Gallimard, 1927) 180. English edition: *Metaphysical Journal* (Chicago: Henry Regnery, 1952).

6. Aelred de Rievaulx, *Le Miroir de la charité,* trans, notes et index by Charles Dumont, ocso, and Gaëtane de Briey, ocso. Vie Monastique 27 (Bégrolles-en-Mauge: Bellefontaine, 1992). A much longer Introduction by Fr. Charles appeared in the English version: Aelred of Rievaulx, *Mirror of Charity,* trans. Elizabeth Connor, ocso. Cistercian Fathers Series 17 (Kalamazoo: Cistercian Publications, 1990).

Now as the months went by, Fr. Charles was occupied with writing reviews for *Collectanea,* especially of articles and books on Thomas Merton. He also went to the south of France for a while to give lectures in some of the monasteries. When he returned Dom Thomas asked him if he could occasionally visit two communities of Carmelite nuns who no longer had chaplains: La Fontaine Olive, near the French border not far from Scourmont, and Mont-sur-Marchienne. To be able to communicate with these sisters in terms of their spirituality Fr. Charles took to reading Saint John of the Cross and found great joy in doing so:

> For God, to gaze upon means to love. This comes up about ten times in the *Spiritual Canticle.* My pleasure in reading Saint John of the Cross no doubt comes especially from the fact that he was a poet and a real poet. Instead of commenting on the *Song of Songs* directly, he composed his own canticle himself, writing almost all of it while he was in prison (Carmelite!) in Toledo. As for me, I am hunting for the style and the *how* for the monastic commentary of the *Song of Songs* I have undertaken. That will be for later on, if God gives me several more years. (2 28.89)

In the midst of all these activities Fr. Charles kept thinking about his project of a synthesis on the spiritual theology of Saint Bernard. It received a boost when his abbot asked him to give a few talks on Saint Bernard to his brother-monks at Scourmont. Anyone who has lived in a monastery knows that speaking in one's own community is the ultimate acid test and that compliments are rare. Fr. Charles meekly had the general impression that his talks went over rather well, but it was only later, after Dom Thomas returned from a visit to his daughter houses in Zaire (Congo Republic), that he learned by a letter from Fr. Albert Derzelle at Mokoto that he—Fr. Charles—had given some remarkable talks to his brothers at Scourmont! In his reply to Fr. Albert, Fr. Charles wrote: "Thank you for telling me what Father Abbot said about my lectures. In community the monks are more reserved."[7] Strengthened by this encouragement, he applied himself even more assiduously to his work on the synthesis.

At Christmas time, while reading Saint Bernard as usual, Fr. Charles' meditation was centered on the Mystery of the interior coming of the Lord, which occurs each day while we wait for our last one *(cras egrediemini)*. On the feast of the Epiphany he turned to Bernard's third sermon for this feast. There, toward the end, the Abbot of Clairvaux spoke of compassionate fraternal charity as being "wine and sober inebriation," just as he did in the fourth degree of the *Treatise on the Love of God* (11.33). This impressed Fr. Charles particularly as being something to make us reflect and to convert us. It was also about this time that he was asked to go over a French translation of Mother Jean-Marie Howe's book *Spiritual Journey. The Monastic Way*,[8] which had been made by a sister of the Paix-Dieu.

> I was surprised to see that Mother Jean-Marie quoted some things I have said just in passing. It always astonishes me that things said offhand like that perhaps come from elsewhere, to touch the heart more than the intelligence. It seems to me that to be present, in the sense that Gabriel Marcel understands this word, one must always be a bit elsewhere, either above or deeper, because if presence is reduced to its spatial-temporal limits, that goes neither very far nor deep . . . (3.3.90)

A passage in Mother Jean-Marie's book made him think of Keats' expression: *negative capability* and prompted him to say: "When a man is capable of living in uncertainties, mysteries and doubts without any irritable reaching after facts and reasons . . . this expression can be applied to a life of faith and, quite simply, to life itself. . . . Patience is everything" (4.24.90).

7. Letter to Fr. Albert Derzelle. June 20, 1990.

8. Mother Jean-Marie Howe, OCSO, *Spiritual Journey. The Monastic Way* (Petersham, MA: St. Bede's Publications, 1989).

The year 1990 marked Fr. Charles' fortieth anniversary of ordination to the priesthood. He looked back over the long road he had traveled: "My ministry as a priest has been interwoven with my life as a monk, and also with friendship. One has to be my age to be able to have an idea of how these things are integrated" (5.26.90). He celebrated the Eucharist at Notre-Dame de la Paix that day which was the feast of the Ascension, and had the pleasant surprise of finding himself encircled by children who were making their profession of faith. At the Our Father each youngster came to shake his hand, and before Communion he gave them the kiss of peace. With his thoughts turned to things above he paraphrased Saint Bernard's fourth sermon *De diversis:* "Seeking God at all times means also waiting for him, so waiting for him at all times. Waiting is a joy, but it makes us suffer, too, when we must renounce more immediately accessible happiness."

At the same time Fr. Charles was working on three more articles. The first, *Thomas Merton, Monk and Literary Critic,* was scheduled to appear in the Belgian periodical: *La Revue Générale.* It was Marcel Lobet, a well-known writer and literary figure in Belgium and long-time friend of Scourmont, who had encouraged Fr. Charles to write and submit this article. In late summer *La Nouvelle Revue Théologique* published his *La Spiritualité de Saint Bernard,*[9] which was like a foretaste of his synthesis that was slowly but surely advancing. The third article came as a response to a question posed by a group of students of Louvain-la-Neuve. They had originally asked Dom Jean Leclercq to interpret for them Saint Benedict's expression *ora et labora*. Dom Leclercq referred them to Fr. Charles who, after going through the *Rule* with a critical eye and consulting the concordance of Saint Bernard's works, saw clearly that although the word *labora* is usually understood to mean the manual work most people identify with the Trappist life, for Saint Bernard it means *dolor* or the affliction and

9. "La Spiritualité de Saint Bernard," in *Nouvelle Revue Théologique* Tome.112/4 1990: 502–515. English: "The Spirituality of Saint Bernard," trans. Patricia Carroll, ocso. *Hallel* 20 (1995) 82–95.

toil of monastic ascesis, and only rarely denotes manual labor.[10] His reply to the students appeared in the periodical *Inter-Mondes.* The following passages drawn from this text bring out both the humanist and Christological implications of this expression of Saint Benedict:

> In the labor essential in the life of every human being, the Christian has the assurance of following God's plan revealed in Christ. While seeking for a culture where our obscure and real reasons for living together are mobilized, the Christian monk can put into practice his faith in the Mystery of the Man-God, just as Saint Bernard did. It is in the union in him of heaven and earth, of the divine and human, that he finds the path of peace, by praying and working . . . .
>
> Is a mystical teaching on work possible? Yes, on condition that the work is integrated (as in Saint Bernard) in the total human experience, from which toil and suffering cannot be subtracted without falsehood and illusion. On the other hand, when work is intimately bound to prayer and united—mysteriously, but very concretely—to God's suffering revealed in Christ, this labor and this toil have an infinite value. Holiness, as Saint Bernard saw it, is humanism saved by God's peace.[11]

Meeting with the Japanese Superiors

The second Mixed General Meeting, concurrent with the Chapters of Abbots and Abbesses, was scheduled to be held in September at Rome. At Bricquebec, in Normandy, a special celebration was to take place before the Chapter to mark both the ninth centenary of Saint Bernard's birth and the first centenary of the entrance at Bricquebec of Dom Vital Lehodey, one of the great spiritual writers of his time. Bricquebec had introduced the Cistercian life in Japan, and the superiors of all the Japanese

10. In the *Concordance* of Saint Bernard's works, *labora* refers to manual labor only 15 times out of 336.

11. "Ora et labora", reproduced later in *Une Éducation du Cœur* (Oka: Abbaye N.-D. du Lac, 1996). Pain de Cîteaux. 3e série, 10) here, 106–107.

houses were to be present at this celebration. For this occasion Fr. Charles was invited to give several talks on Saint Bernard. It was the first time he had ever spoken to Japanese monks and nuns and he thoroughly enjoyed this new experience.

As time went on, a number of French abbots and abbesses were encouraging Fr. Charles to make his synthesis on Saint Bernard's spirituality available to them. About this same time the Canadian monasteries had been asking him to come for lectures. So more than fifteen years after his last visit to North America he made plans to return to Canada in September, 1991.[12] This permitted him to try out his bernardine synthesis on the Cistercian communities in Quebec and New Brunswick. His typewritten text now numbered about a hundred pages, with the margins full of scribbled-in texts or quotations ranging from Scripture to Paul Valéry. On the back of one page of the sixth chapter, Fr. Charles had xeroxed a card with a short passage in calligraphy by Sr. Monique Simon of the Paix-Dieu, one of the students at the 1972 Chimay trimester. The text was from Saint Bernard's 26th sermon *de Diversis:* "It is our consent which we must submit to the divine will, if we desire to arrive at eternal peace as well as peace during this present life."[13] As in Europe, the response to his lectures in Canada was encouraging. While he was at Oka, one of the monks suggested to Fr. Charles that he should have his lectures published in book form. Fr. André Picard, editor of Pain de Cîteaux, was also present at the lectures and welcomed the suggestion. He told Fr. Charles that his book could be published whenever his text would be ready.

On the title page of his manuscript he added three more monasteries to the list of houses in which he had presented his progressing work. At Saint Romuald he met another monk-poet, Fr. Yves Girard, of Oka. Fr. Charles had first seen Fr. Yves' books in Belgium and had felt himself to be on the same wave

12. Fr. Charles had also been invited by Dom Thomas Davis, abbot of New Clairvaux, to teach philosophy for a year at Vina. It was not possible for him to accept such a long-term course.

13. Bernard of Clairvaux, Div 26.4. *Sancti Bernardi Opera* VI-1: 196–197.

length. As he once said, "Only a poet can really understand another poet."

After lecturing in the Canadian monasteries, Fr. Charles went on to Chicago to see his nephew, Christian De Vos, who was studying to become a permanent deacon. Fr. Charles had the opportunity to accompany Christian and his wife Marnie to a Scripture class given by a young Dominican. "It was on Abraham, quite different from the kind of course Fr. Maur gives. It was a little bit like he was a commentator of a football game, but it was the real thing, and he was avidly listened to" (10.2.91). Since his birthday was coming up in a few days, his nephew and niece invited him to dinner with some friends at the restaurant on the ninety-fifth floor of the Hancock Center. The view of the myriad lights of the city was fairylike, but looking down from such a height made Fr. Charles dizzy!

Lessons on Saint Bernard

During this whole period, just as during his first years of teaching at Caldey, Fr. Charles gave himself unstintingly to the formation of the monks and nuns he met in the various monasteries. Never overbearingly didactic, always encouraging and helpful, he was a sure guide for those who sought his assistance for their studies or spiritual life. Many became his friends. His belief in and love for the Cistercian life was catching and led others to follow the way traced by the Cistercian Fathers. As Fr. Charles became progressively aware of the need and thirst in the monasteries for solid formation in Cistercian spirituality and theology, he decided to undertake a correspondence course for anyone who would like to explore the heritage of the Order. The following lines are taken from the introductory circular letter he sent out to fifty monasteries:

> As I was to give a course in the novitiate at Scourmont and lectures at both Soleilmont and Chimay, and because some brothers and sisters have asked me to help them with their

> *lectio divina* in the works of Saint Bernard, it seemed to me to be useful to study texts which have special significance in his doctrine and his way of presenting it. The choice of texts follows the order of the six chapters of the bernardine synthesis I drew up last year,[14] and which I have presented since then in several communities of the Order . . . There could be an exchange (of ideas) by correspondence, at more or less regular intervals . . . There will be neither examinations nor a diploma . . . Not all the questions suggested in these lessons require a reply; when they do, the answers can be either more or less developed and in a free style. Parallels with contemporary authors, religious or profane, would be stimulating and would give present-day meaning to a type of language often foreign to contemporary sensibility. Personal reflection on acquired knowledge, and especially on experience in the spiritual and monastic life, or simply in one's own life, will be likewise profitable for everyone . . . While I was meditating on this project on the feast of Saint Anthony, the father of monks, I read the following passage: "He spoke to them in Egyptian: The Scriptures are really sufficient for our instruction. Yet it is well for us to encourage one another in the faith, and to employ words to stimulate ourselves. You, therefore, be like children and bring to your father what you know and tell it, while I, your senior, share with you my knowledge and my experience. Let us all have the same zeal, not to give up what we have begun, not to lose heart (because of the effort)."[15]

In this letter he explained the approach he was going to use, and inserted as an appendix a text by Dom Bernardo Olivera, the new Abbot General of the Order, on different *ways of access* to Saint Bernard's works. Dom Bernardo had divided these ways into two categories: scientific and nonscientific. For his lessons, Fr. Charles chose a nonscientific approach: *evaluative-existential*. This approach "confronts the permanent values found in Saint

14. . . . but not yet in its definitive form.

15. Circular letter, January, 1991. See Saint Athanasius, *Life of Saint Anthony* 16. Trans. Robert T. Meyer (Westminster, MD: Newman Press, 1950) 33–34.

Bernard's works with contemporary values, discerns what is obsolete and reintroduces language corresponding to the categories of understanding of people today."[16]

The lessons, entitled simply *Notes intended to be helpful for reading Saint Bernard* were from time to time accompanied by a letter addressed to "Disciples of Saint Bernard" or "Dear brothers and sisters in Saint Bernard." They sometimes gave instructions concerning the subject matter to be dealt with in the lesson or made a link between the lesson and the current period of the liturgical year. At one point he sent out copies of a long article on methodology by Fr. Pierre-André Burton, who at that time was a junior professed monk at Scourmont: *Why is it difficult to read the Cistercian Fathers? An attempt to reply and a plan for a method.* There was no fixed time limit for each lesson. Each student could advance at his or her own pace, so that anyone wishing to delve deeper into a certain subject could do so before continuing with the following lesson.

By the middle of 1990, the ninth centenary of Saint Bernard's birth, twelve students were sending their replies to him regularly. Fr. Charles added the following letter as an annex to the Ninth Lesson:

> To become an apostle of Saint Bernard always presupposes a certain conversion, as it was with me. But once a person is captivated by this one develops a taste for it, and that is the goal of these lessons with their questions: to focus attention and awaken interest, so that finally one develops a taste for it.[17]

After more than two years of experience with this project, in a circular letter sent out on All Saints Day, 1993, Fr. Charles listed the subject matter which had been dealt with so far in the lessons:

16. See Bernardo Olivera, "Para une lectura de las obras de San Bernardo," in *Cuadernos Monasticos* 94 (1990) 287–306.

17. Circular letter to students. August 20, 1991.

Lessons 1–7: Sermon 85 *On the Song of Songs;*
Lessons 8–12: Sermons 34–38 *On the Song of Songs* (on real knowledge and ignorance);
Lessons 13–14: Sermon 50 *On the Song of Songs* (affective and effective charity);
Lesson 15: Sermon 23 *On the Song of Songs* (from active charity to contemplation);
Lesson 16: What is Consideration?
Lesson 17: Sermon 14 *On the Song of Songs* (excursus on friendship);
Lesson 18: Sermons for Advent: the three comings;
Lesson 19: Two Sermons for Septuagesima;
Lesson 20: Sermons for Lent (2 and 3);
Lesson 21: Sermons *On Psalm 90* (1, 2, 4, 5, 7, 8, 9, 14, 15, 17);
Lesson 22: Sermon 4 for the Ascension;
Lesson 23: Three sermons for Saint Andrew (the cross and joy);
Lesson 24–25: Sermons for the Lord's Nativity.

By then the lessons were being translated into English, Spanish, Dutch and Italian. Although a number of would-be students had not put themselves to the task because they "didn't have time!" twenty Cistercian and Bernardine nuns—plus one American hermitess—were persevering in the program. Fr. Charles had a ten-inch pile of replies on his desk. Some students had "answered all the questions, others preferred to change the order of the exercises; for many the effort has been rewarded by a better understanding of Saint Bernard and often with an enthusiasm of which I have been the primary beneficiary. The papers could be used as material for a florilegium."[18] Soon after, however, in a Christmas letter to the students he wrote that it was time to interrupt the course "to allow the laggards to catch up on their work and also to permit me to finish my synthesis of the Cistercian spirituality of Saint Bernard

18. Circular letter to "faithful disciples of this course and of Saint Bernard," December 12, 1993.

(the school of charity) that the editor is waiting for." To conclude this letter, as his Christmas greeting to the students he quoted the last phrase from Saint Bernard's fifth sermon for Christmas:

> A Saviour is born for us today!
> The angel did not speak of "night."
> In fact, "night is far advanced, day is very near" (Rm 13:12).
> Yes, the true day came from the Day,
> God's salvation, Jesus Christ.

. . . and Philosophy

At one point Fr. Charles had inquired if anyone would like to follow a similar course on Aelred. The response was quite affirmative, but various circumstances prevented him from undertaking such a project. Rather, during the summer of 1991 he did begin a philosophy course entitled. *Contemplative existentialism or Cistercian wisdom*. No questions were added to these lessons. They consisted simply of texts meant to stimulate reflection. Kierkegaard, Gabriel Marcel, Henri Bergson, M. Heidegger, Paul Claudel, Cardinal Newman, Aimé Forest and others were often quoted. The plan for an introduction to philosophy drawn up by Fr. Thomas Litt, Fr. Charles' first philosophy professor, was added to the fourth lesson. Only five lessons—or *Considerations* as he called them—appeared, but they are very substantial. His intention in diffusing these pages was expressed in his Presentation of the first lesson:

> The (pages that follow) are simply notes from my times of *lectio* during fifty years of Cistercian life. I have taken them from my notebooks and file cards. Some of them, written on paper that has become yellow with age or with ink that has dried out, are hardly legible at all. The only unity that exists among these notes is that they were transcribed, underlined and chosen by me. On one of my notebooks I wrote: *Plus eligere quam legere*. One day when Dom Anselme Le Bail was in the scriptorium and happened to pass by my desk, he saw this and made me the sign: "that's good." It is a bit in memory of him that I begin this course, by dedicating

> it to the one who was my first abbot and who encouraged me in this type of *lectio*. For ten years my obedience was to teach philosophy; then during the next ten years I was asked to give courses in patrology. The second step was not unrelated to the first, because it is easy to see that philosophy had a strong influence on Christian teaching: the wisdom of the Stoics during the first three centuries, and in the fourth century through the Platonism of the Cappadocian Fathers and Saint Augustine. Much later, Saint Thomas and scholasticism were predominately influenced by Aristotle. There is also a tradition which sees the Christian as *the* true philosopher; the Cistercians adopted this tradition.[19]

In passing, it could be pointed out that in his Preface to the *Mirror of Charity* Aelred of Rievaulx had explained that he composed his book from notes taken during his reading, inserting the selected passages where it seemed best. Fr. Charles used the same method, generally speaking. Also, as a companion piece to his course he wrote a paper entitled: *Notes on Aelred's philosophical categories*. In both we find the same orientation that is found throughout Cistercian literature: insistence on wisdom and love, and the wisdom of love. For example, the third Consideration is entitled: *Play, to contemplate wisdom;* the fourth: *Anyone who abides in friendship abides in God*. He passes from Plato to Thomas Merton with ease without the erudition being unpalatable.

As Fr. Charles explained when he sent out the first lesson: "(Your professor) has no diploma. Like everybody else, he began his philosophical career at the age of three or four when he began to ask 'why?' all the time. Fortunately he is still asking the same question, because what is essential in philosophical thought is our astonishment before the fact that things are what they are, and this is a source of continual joy." When he was preparing his course, it was indeed a joy and delight for Fr. Charles to go back over the first lectures he had given at Caldey in 1951: "At

19. See C. Dumont, "Humanisme et Rusticité," *Cîteaux* 31 (1980) 21–34. Trans. Richard Summers, ocso, "Humanism and Rusticity. Aim and Practice of the Early Cistercians," *Cistercian Studies* XVII (1982) 65–81.

that time I was writing *beeing* instead of being and, after all, that is what I have been doing all my life: *'butiner,'* gathering *nova et vetera* from flower to flower like a bee, across the fields of thought."

Other activities were also occupying Fr. Charles. For one thing, he had to get to work seriously on material on Saint Bernard and the Blessed Virgin Mary to be presented at the *Faculté des Religions et des Humanismes laïques* of the Inter-University Center for Formation, in Charleroi.[20] These talks, scheduled for the middle of January, required careful preparation because he was to speak to Christians and non-Christians, agnostics and atheists. He chose as title: *Saint Bernard, monk, poet and mystic of Our Lady.* In his first lecture, he entered into his subject with soft steps:

> I thank you for inviting me to speak to you about Saint Bernard and what he thought, meditated and wrote on the Virgin Mary. I must first tell you that I come as a monk, without any university qualification. So I will speak about doctrinal theology only to the extent that it helps us to situate Saint Bernard and understand what he sang, prayed and contemplated. . . . It is that Bernard whom I am going to present to you, hoping that you will love him . . . Before plunging into the subject, let me quote Solzhenitsyn. The scene is a woman history professor in Moscow explaining her course to the Marxist girls in her class: "To reject the Middle Ages means to break up western history, and then nothing comprehensible remains in the contemporary fragment . . . So what was more important? Oh, if you want to know what was most important during the Middle Ages, it is the spiritual life, a spiritual life of such intensity that it outweighs material existence, so that humanity has never known anything like it either before or after."[21]

20. First published under the title "Marie, la Mère de Jésus" in *Cahiers de la FORel*. Faculté des Religions et des Humanismes Laïques (Charleroi: 1992) 59–80. Later in *Une éducation du Cœur*, 153–189.

21. Idem. Quoting A. Solzhenitsyn, *August 14*. Trans. H. T. Willetts (N.Y.: Farrar, Straus and Giroux, 1989) ch. 58.

Fr. Charles went on to develop the various aspects of Saint Bernard's Mariology. A few days after his first talk, he wrote to a friend: "Several of those who were sitting in front of me were taking notes on Saint Bernard and the Virgin Mary!" As always when he gave lectures in new places, he came away with new friends.

After Easter Fr. Charles undertook the organization of a task that had become very necessary: computerizing the Tables of the *Bulletin de Spiritualité Monastique,* from the first issue of *Collectanea* until the current issue. To facilitate the work of those who would participate on this project, he consulted the directors of the *Nouvelle Revue Théologique,* known for its very extensive bibliographies. At the same time, he was also writing an article on action and contemplation which he had been turning over in his mind for forty years.[22] As it happened, while he was working on it he ran across an article by David Schindler, a professor at Notre Dame University, entitled *Time in Eternity, and Eternity in Time,*[23] which corresponded to the idea of time found in Saint Bernard. Needless to say, Fr. Charles was delighted. He commented on this article: "It is all based on T. S. Eliot, and confirmed by Balthasar . . . The link between action and contemplation, which is the link of time embodied in suffering, sacrifice and the cross of Christ, is also the meaning of the monastic life . . ." (2.16.91).

More Lectures and Workshops

After Easter, 1992, Fr. Charles set out for another workshop on Saint Bernard in Italy, this time at Vitorchiano. It was to be a follow-up of the formators' previous meeting at Tre Fontane,

22. "L'action contemplative, le temps dans l'éternité, d'après Saint Bernard." This article appeared first in *La Foi et le Temps* 21 (1991) 307–324, then in *Collectanea* 54 (1992) 269–283. It was reprinted in *Une Education du Coeur* 57–77. Trans. P. Carroll, ocso, and C. Heaney, ocso: "Contemplative Action: Time in Eternity according to Saint Bernard," *Cistercian Studies Quarterly* XXVIII (1993) 145–159.

23. David Schindler, "Time in Eternity, Eternity in Time: On the Contemplative Life," *Communio* 18.1 (1991) 53–68.

but with an enlarged group. Approximately seventy monks and nuns from Vitorchiano, Valserena, Saint Suzanna, OC (Rome), San Bernardo, OC (Rome), Boschi, Frattochie and Tre Fontane attended. Fr. Charles also met with the novice masters and mistresses during the workshop. Afterwards, he wrote: "Of two hundred formation meetings, this was one of the best. . . . I came back (to Scourmont) delighted, optimistic, and exhausted. . . . I am getting my strength back little by little" (5.16.92).

Days of Study on Aelred of Rievaulx's Mirror of Charity

Dom Thomas resigned as abbot of Scourmont in 1992 and was succeeded by Fr. Gerard Van Gheluwe, who became superior ad nutum in February and was elected abbot of Scourmont the following July. Dom Gerard asked Fr. Charles to take charge of the juniors and, a little later on, the novitiate. With one junior professed and two postulants he had plenty to keep him busy, but at the same time another project was coming into focus. The French translation of the *Speculum caritatis* had just come off the press. Fr. Charles wanted to organize some kind of a meeting to study this veritable manual for monastic life. With the assistance of Sr. Gaëtane he planned what they called *Days of Study on Saint Aelred of Rievaulx,* to be held October 5–9, 1992, at Scourmont. Fr. Charles saw this project as a kind of preparation for the coming Mixed General Meeting and General Chapters of the Order which were to have as the theme: *Cistercian Contemplative Identity.* "The *Mirror of Charity* is symbolic of the school of charity, and my intention is to give the Chapter some hint of our patrimony . . . The more I read the *Mirror,* the more I see how much this final goal of charity orientates everything in the Cistercian life and identifies it. It is contemplation: active charity. There is no other on this earth!" (4.3.92).

Several weeks before the Days of Study Fr. Charles left with Br. Pierre-André for Caldey, where he was to be the resource person at a meeting for novice directors of the Region of the Isles. Before the meeting, however, they went to Ireland to visit Bolton and Glencairn. There Fr. Charles fell ill with a bad migraine "so that I was magnificently and tenderly cared for—the Irish way! They say that in Ireland to be constantly happy you must be in distress all the time!" (5.16.92). When he was quite well again he and Br. Pierre-André set out for Caldey. On their peregrinations they had long discussions which included, of course, the subject of contemplative identity:

> As regards the challenge of modern mentality, this is a very confusing term—not because of the translation but because of the very idea! Why should we compete with worldly values—that's out of date! We have been intimidated during the last twenty years by worldly values . . . This is not the language of the first two chapters of the *First Letter to the Corinthians*. The two wisdoms are not on the same wave length. (4.3.92)

Visiting Caldey always brought back memories. The sea, especially, enchanted him. Enjoying some solitude on the island he wrote a poem, one of the few he wrote in English:

Waves, Holy Waves

O the waves by night
So calmly kissing
The sand of my life.

Majestic drum of time
Bordering silence eternal.

O gentle silver edge
Slowly gliding on my past,
Compassionate waves
Take away the sins of the world.

Ocean of love
Sea of boundless heart
By the fingers of your tender waves
Touch my restless mind,

Grant us peace[24]

24. "*Waves, Holy Waves*," printed in *Hallel* 18 (1993) 123. Reprinted in *Poèmes et Prières*, 102.

On the way home, Fr. Charles and Br. Pierre-André stopped in London. Then with friends they set out for Rievaulx. Although Fr. Charles had criss-crossed England often, going back and forth between Scourmont and Caldey, he had never before been to Yorkshire. At Rievaulx he walked at last on soil which Aelred had trod, looked out over the encircling hills that Aelred had lived among and, especially, celebrated the Eucharist where the altar had been, in the ruins of the Church, in this very place where Aelred had sung the Office and celebrated the Memorial of the Lord with his monks. Later he said, "I expected to meet him in the cloisters or the chapter house" (Oct. 92).

The response to the announcement for the Days of Study exceeded his expectations. Monks and nuns from several countries, including several abbots and abbesses, as well as a number of lay scholars signed up, so that even the spacious guesthouse at Scourmont could not lodge everyone. At a time when so many meetings included dialogues, this one was organized differently: five days of lectures, morning and afternoon. The talks could be classified as follows: 1. Introduction; 2. The *Mirror*-Analyses; 3. The *Mirror*—Syntheses; 4. Aelred the historian; 5. Aelred the Poet; 6. Conclusion. Besides Fr. Charles, who gave two talks, the speakers included Fr. Gaetano Raciti, of Orval, the American Cistercian scholar Marsha Dutton, Sr. Gaëtane de Briey of Clairefontaine, Sr. Imelda of Igny, Fr. James McEvoy of Maynooth (who was studying at Louvain at the time and was a frequent visitor at Scourmont), Sr. Olga Horvath of Kismaros in Hungary, Brothers Gabriel Ghislain and Pierre André Burton of Scourmont, and Sr. Elizabeth Connor of Saint Romuald. Unfortunately, Fr. Maur Standaert's health prevented him from giving the conference for which he was scheduled. The last afternoon Dom Gerard Dubois gave a masterful summary-conclusion of these days of study. Some participants felt that these days were like a retreat. When someone remarked that there were no discussions, another participant replied that there was no need for discussions because everyone was in agreement. He meant, of course, that everyone agreed with Aelred's teaching. One might say that it was like verbal *lectio:* listening to what Aelred had taught, and letting it fall on receptive soil in one's mind and heart. There were lots of conversations during meals and free time, in the guest house cloister flooded with mellow autumn sunlight, or in the garden still in bloom.

One of the most memorable moments during the Days of Study occurred on the last day. Dom Anselme Hoste, Fr. Charles' fellow Aelred scholar and old friend, had been invited to the meeting but was able to come only for this one day. He arrived just before dinner and was shown directly to the refectory. For some reason or other Fr. Charles was not at dinner that day, but during the middle of the meal the usual buzz of conversation all at once faded until there was complete silence. Then someone whispered: Père Charles! And, in fact, Fr. Charles had come into the refectory and was quietly making his way across the room toward Dom Anselme, who rose to greet him. The two monks embraced. It was a golden moment; these two monks had shared so many things through the years. Fr. Charles said later, "Dom Anselme and I have had only one disagreement, and that was about friendship!" meaning, of course, their different interpretations of certain passages in Aelred's treatise *On Friendship.*

In their free time during those days the participants could look at the photos taken during Fr. Charles' recent visit to Rievaulx. That, too, made up part of the subject matter. The homily during the closing Eucharistic celebration was given by Fr. Amadée Hallier, whose book *Aelred of Rievaulx, Monastic Educator* remains a classic.[25] Afterwards, Fr. Charles reminisced about the days of yore when Fr. Amadée was doing research for this book in Scourmont's library and enlisted young Fr. Charles' help in classifying his file cards . . . his first step in studies on Aelred!

The complete texts from the Days of Study, which make up an impressive dossier on Aelred, were published in a special

25. Amadée Hallier, ocso, *Un éducateur monastique: Aelred de Rievaulx,* (Paris: J. Gabalda, 1959). Trans. Columban Heaney, ocso, *The Monastic Theology of Aelred of Rievaulx.* Cistercian Studies Series 2 (Spencer: Cistercian Publications, 1969).

double issue of *Collectanea* which the editor, Fr. Yvon Petit, offered in *Hommage au P. Charles Dumont*.[26]

Toward Poyo

At their meeting at Gethsemani in June, 1992, the Central Commissions of the Order had voted to invite Fr. Charles as an expert to the next Mixed General Meeting which was to take place at Poyo, Spain, in September, 1993. He was also one of four persons asked to contribute a Working Paper on the theme of the Meeting: *Cistercian Contemplative Identity*. Every point Fr. Charles dealt with in his document was a stimulant for reflection and lent itself to discussion, as a working paper should. As always, he insisted on the primacy of the spiritual as foundation of the monastic life. The following ample quotations from this valuable document reflect Fr. Charles' vision of the Order:

First of all: Explanation of the terminology:

> **I.**1. **Contemplative identity.** "The Cistercian Order is a monastic Institute wholly ordered to contemplation" (C. 2). We could also use the word "ordered" as the beginning of our research.
>
> **I.**2. It is therefore unnecessary to go back to the Greek philosophers, or to the history of the distinction between action/contemplation up to our time, passing through the radical modification brought about by evangelical monasticism. We might prefer the term "spiritual," understanding the word "spirituality" by the concrete form manifested in our Cistercian life by the teaching of the Gospel.
>
> **I.**3. **Identity . . .** There is no crisis of identity. Our identity has not been lost in our controversies over the means, even if these debates have often caused us to lose sight of our end: the spiritual life to which everything else is directed. It is rather a question of renewing our esteem for the primacy

26. *Collectanea* 55 (1993) 1 & 2.

of the spiritual and deepening this sense within ourselves and in our communities. Moreover, this is what we have been doing since the beginning of the Order. . . .

I.4. This deepening of our vocation could advantageously take the form which Saint Bernard called "consideration." It could be a reflection on the experience of our concrete existence. It is therefore not a question of various theories or conflicts of interpretation, but rather of a conversion as community, in process and never finished.

I.5. The term **identity** also signifies the continuity of a being in time. A social being can only be perpetuated within a tradition. But a spiritual tradition is not transmitted like an object. It is not received unless it is welcomed as a gift, as Gabriel Marcel has so aptly said.[27] The Cistercian patrimony will be ours only if we receive it with gratitude, respect and *pietas,* which for Saint Bernard is the definition itself of consideration.[28] The spirit of religious gratitude allows us to transcend in a mysterious way both time and culture, connecting us directly to the origin of our personal and communal vocation.

Fr. Charles then presented several other aspects of the question, particularly the deepening of understanding of the Cistercian patrimony (**III**), but also the question of the Young Churches (**V**):

III.6. It is perhaps helpful in our present concern to clearly understand what Saint Bernard means by love within the framework of monastic conversion. It concerns essentially a deep intentional concurrence of the human will with the divine will. This harmony of wills **is** union with God. This intent of the will, understood throughout the tradition as inclination of the heart, ability to love, is always active and requires acts, evidence of love, which will at the same time

27. Cf. Gabriel Marcel, *Le declin de la Sagesse* (Paris: Plon, 1954). See pages 43–75. English edition: *Decline of Wisdom* (Chicago: Philosophical Library, Inc., 1955).

28. Bernard of Clairvaux, *On Consideration* I.8. *Sancti Bernardi Opera* III:403.

> be its trials. Austerity and observance is therefore desired for the sake of love and love is sustained through the observance. This articulation of the ascesis of contemplation is therefore rather specific while also being fundamentally traditional. All praxis is contemplative because it is always for love and therefore in union with God.
>
> The spiritual dimension therefore envelops all activity as well as a charity which is actual (in acts: *actualis*). This is diversified according to the demands of a life engaged in the domain of the Spirit (*spiritualia: lectio,* meditation, consideration) and in more external activities (*corporalia*); work, silence, sobriety, fasts, vigils. The Christology of Saint Bernard, the basis of his theology, is marked by this care to justify an incarnational spirituality.[29]
>
> **V.**1. The expansion of the Order has created the possibility for an enrichment of its spiritual life thanks to the variety of the cultures by which the Cistercian patrimony has been received and assimilated. In fact this possibility has not yet been clearly perceived and therefore has not been fully utilized.

He posed the question of whether the contribution of the Young Churches should not be "mutual and reciprocal," and went on to say:

> **V.**3. The inculturation of the Cistercian patrimony is not a question that concerns only the Young Churches. Dom Bernardo Olivera wrote an article, years ago, with a conclusion in eleven points that can contribute a great deal of light to all. We can only refer to it at this point.[30] Almost all the points of that synthesis insist on the prime importance of welcoming the patrimony without any reserve. In relationship to the present research, it is evident that the spiritual or

29. See C. Dumont, "The Spirituality of Saint Bernard," *Nouvelle Revue Théologique* 112 (1990) 502–515. Trans. Patricia Carroll, ocso, *Hallel* 20 (1995) 82–95.

30. Bernardo Olivera, ocso, "Propos sur l'inculturation du patrimoine cistercien," *Bulletin A.I.M.* (1985, no. 39) 46–48.

> contemplative dimension of Cistercian life has to be found in the first place in the content of that patrimony. A mutual exchange of the Cistercian experience and thought can be realized only from an anterior mutual agreement on the primacy of the spiritual.
>
> **V.**4. The problems that emerge from the development of culture concern all the Churches. They were faced in a splendid manner at Vatican II in Chapter 11 of the Constitution *Gaudium et Spes*. It is human culture in general, and Christian humanism in particular, that are threatened, as is well indicated in the following sentence: "As special branches of knowledge continue to shoot out so rapidly, how can the necessary synthesis of them be worked out, and how can men preserve the ability to contemplate and to wonder, from which wisdom comes?" (II, 56, 4). Is there not in that sentence an indication concerning intellectual formation in our monasteries and a call to our responsibility as contemplatives?

In the closing part of his paper (**VI**), Fr. Charles dealt with the challenges of contemporary mentality, pointing out that

> **VI.**3. The greatest difficulty that is felt nowadays, rather differently from one place to another, however, is the disappearance of religious preoccupation in contemporary society . . . What can poverty, chastity and obedience for the Kingdom of God mean, if this kingdom does not exist? It would be pretentious to imagine that in such a climate the temptation to look for compensations or evasions is not stronger and more insidious than in the past . . . Monastic values will assume a different nature under this same "worldly" influence. "Are all the elements of our Cistercian life still really subordinated to its contemplative dimension, or have they reached a form of autonomy? For example, work becomes economy; *lectio* becomes study, hospitality becomes pastoral."[31]

31. *Minutes* of the Netherlands Regional Meeting (Brecht: O.L. of Nazareth Abbey, 1992) 6.

> **VI**.4. It is superfluous trying to justify the contemplative dimension of our life with human sciences as many tried to do during the nineteen sixties. More radically and more concretely would it not be good to note with Saint Paul that "the natural man does not accept what is taught by the Spirit of God . . . The spiritual man, on the other hand, can appraise everything, though he himself can be appraised by no one" (1 Cor. 2.14-15). But the natural man is in us . . . An interpretation of these verses would be challenging in the present situation.
>
> As for post-modernity . . .
>
> **VI**.5.a. (It) is less a school of thought than perplexity before a culture which deified itself to the point of declaring that God is dead. It recovers the kingdom of human experience in its deepest dimension: its ultimate question concerning the meaning of life. The multiplication of the branches of knowledge mentioned by *Gaudium et Spes* (Ch. 2) led to the disrepute of academic knowledge and especially of sociology concerning spiritual anthropology. Hence the comfort given by this form of thought whose newness does not reside any more in technical and rational progress, but in a new interior space, that of the contemplative dimension.[32]

Fr. Charles concluded his paper with references to two twentieth-century thinkers:

> **VI**.5.b. Some ask themselves what contribution we can bring to our contemporary society. Reading Henri Bergson's beautiful book again, and specially his final remarks on *Mechanics and Mysticism,* in chapter IV,[33] I thought that his description

32. Here Fr. Charles inserted a reference to Cardinal J. M. Lustiger's talk: "The newness of Christ and post-modernity," published in *Observatore Romano* (January 30, 1990), which gave a brief presentation of post-modernity, showing its place in the history of modern thought.

33. Henri Bergson, *Les deux sources de la morale et de la religion* (Paris: Alcan, 1932) 287–343. English edition: *The Two Sources of Morality and Religion* (Indiana: University of Notre Dame Press, 1994).

of contemporary mentality was still more up to date than sixty years ago (with the exception of the word "consumerism," invented later). The remedy that he proposes is also one which many people who suffer from being enclosed in a one-dimensional world have a presentiment of and to which they aspire. "A return to a certain simplicity of life—said Bergson—is not unthinkable. Science could very well open the way to it for us."[34] Is it necessary to recall that such a simplicity was put forward as the characteristic aspect of Cîteaux? A brief formula from Saint Bernard expresses the Cistercian ideal in every field: "Reject what is superfluous and you are saved!"[35] . . . A man who was a witness to what is best in contemporary atheistic mentality put out this challenge: "What is happiness if not the simple accord between a person and his existence?"[36] Should we not take this "simple accord" into consideration? Could we not do it with the Blessed Virgin Mary and all the Blessed, and in every dimension: breadth, height, length and depth (cf. Eph. 3.18)?[37]

After he had put the finishing touch on this Working Paper, Fr. Charles turned to other things. He reflected: "My three recent compositions: the lectures for the Caldey meeting, the working paper for the General Chapter and the talks for the Days of Study could form one single document. I could put all that together in an existential synthesis, but I will have to work it up and it is quite difficult" (9.4.92). What he did instead was to write an article on the renewal of Cistercian identity in the light of Thomas Merton's thought, for a special issue of *Collectanea* marking the twenty-fifth anniversary of Merton's death. This article cannot

34. Ibid., 324.

35. Bernard of Clairvaux, See *Sermons on the Song of Songs* 58.10. *Sancti Bernardi Opera* II:134.

36. Albert Camus, *Noces (le désert)* (Paris: Gallimard, NRF, 1950) 85.

37. The above quotations are all from "Cistercian Contemplative Identity." English version of the Booklet of Working Papers for the General Chapters at Poyo in 1993, 23–32.

be commented on at length here, but if we were to choose one phrase from Merton quoted in it, we could take this one: "The specific value which draws a Christian to the 'desert' and 'solitude' is the profound sense that *God alone suffices*."[38] Toward the beginning of this same article Fr. Charles described a dream he had one night during the Poyo Chapter. It illustrates quite well how he felt about legislative structures and the primacy of the spiritual life. Let us first say that before leaving for the General Chapter in Spain he had slipped a copy of *Don Quixote* into his travelling bag:

> During the last Chapter, which took place in Spain, I had a dream of Merton making a speech in the Chapter aula. Would the tight agenda of the Chapter have allowed time for such a Don Quixote? Or perhaps Sancho Panza—who was also in him—would have spoken for him with his brusque humor, telling us: "Don't harbour any illusions: your identity does not rest in any decrees and statutes passed by authority; on the other hand, the danger of irresponsibility and shallowness, of hazardous innovations, is also real. The true strength of monasticism is to be sought in its capacity for renunciation, silence, prayer, faith, and its conviction about the value of the Cross in our life. All genuine renewal must seek life at the source of life: the Cross and Resurrection of Jesus Christ." And the Moderator of the assembly would have politely thanked him and then moved on to the next point on the program.[39]

Actually, Fr. Charles spoke in public only a few times during the Chapter, but as often is the case informal contacts were sometimes more important than what was said in plenary sessions. His presence at the Chapter also gave him the occasion to meet

38. Charles Dumont, "Thomas Merton: pour le renouveau de l'identité cistercienne," *Collectanea* 56 (1994) 11–20; quoting *passim Contemplation in a World of Action* (Garden City, NY: Doubleday Image Books, 1973) 29–30. Trans. Nicholas Groves, "Cistercian Identity Today: Revisiting Thomas Merton," *Cistercian Studies Quarterly* 33 (1998) 487–498.

39. Ibid., 12.

with Madre Cecilia, of Hinojo, who had invited him to come to Argentina to give some lectures. Together they worked out plans for his journey which would take him also to Chile.

Several weeks after his return to Scourmont, he received a letter from a member of the Chapter, one of those who had presented a conference at Poyo:

> It's your feast-day (November 4), and I am happy to send my best wishes, by this little note and especially in the heart of the Eucharist, with all the joy that comes from our meeting (at the Chapter).
>
> Yes, I appreciated your presence as 'expert' at this Chapter. Your silence said by way of contrast that we didn't stay with our principal theme very long. It is especially on this subject that I would have liked to talk to you . . . Thanks also for sending me your *Existential contemplative philosophy*. It whets my appetite for what went before and what will come after . . . Can we prolong our dialogue that way, and our comprehension?
>
> When I came back, I told the brothers that I would like to have you come to give some talks. But we are so far away and such a small group . . . Don't take your age as a pretext! At present there are other reasons which make us postpone inviting anyone. But, would you agree to the idea? Once again, may Saint Charles keep you in his care. And accept my respectful gratitude, which is also affectionate communion.

This letter was signed by the prior of O. L. of Atlas, Dom Christian de Chergé. In the light of later tragic events at Atlas, one can understand what "the other reasons" were for him not to invite Fr. Charles at that time.

6

AFTER 50 YEARS OF MONASTIC LIFE . . .

> *Ruth stayed with Boaz' servants until the harvest of barley and of wheat was finished.* (Rt 2:23)

Golden Jubilee

July 2, 1993, marked Fr. Charles' Golden Jubilee of Profession. It had been a long time since at Momignies, where the community had taken refuge during the war, Dom Anselme had received his first vows on the feast of the Visitation, 1943. On this special day Fr. Charles presided at the concelebration at Scourmont and gave the homily. Because it is so typical of the monk this book is about, it seems apropos to transcribe it here, as well as the Prayer of the Faithful which followed:

> When Father Abbot invited me to give the homily this morning, it seemed to me that I heard the Abbot who received me pose the question: *What do you ask?* After fifty years of monastic profession can a monk answer anything else but what he replied when he made his first vows: *The mercy of God and of the Order?* Still, there is a difference between saying these words when one is twenty-five years old, and fifty years later when one is seventy-five. Between the two there is a long experience of this mercy. For what concerns God's mercy, that is my secret and his. For what concerns the mercy of the Order, that is to say, of the community, that isn't a secret for anyone. Even before my profession, when I

was presented for the vote a senior monk got up and said: "If we give him butter for breakfast already, what will it be like later on?" To elaborate on all the indulgence of which I have been the object would be to tell the story of my life and for that you would not forgive me. I will simply and briefly explain my reasons for the choice of today's readings and music which bring very old memories to my mind . . . The reading from the second chapter of the *Book of Ruth* reminds me of the words I asked to have printed on the card commemorating my first profession: "She stayed with Boaz' servants until the harvest of barley and of wheat was finished" (Rt 2:23). In 1938 a commentary by a nineteenth-century abbot, Tardif de Moidrey, on the moral sense of the *Book of Ruth* was published. Paul Claudel's laudatory introduction to this book included a development on the figurative sense of Scripture. There was also a long chapter on preparation for religious profession. At that moment when I was getting ready to renounce everything, during my retreat before profession under the guidance of Fr. Corneille at the château of Beauchamp, *voilà* the assistant Novice Master, Fr. Francis Mahieu, gave me this text. Claudel was not very well thought of in the field of Scripture studies at that time, but today we find him quoted by Br. Gabriel in *Collectanea* and by Professor Adoph Gesché even in the erudite *Revue Théologique de Louvain.* To come back to Ruth, if Boaz is truly the figure of Christ, the one who has the right to redeem, the story becomes very meaningful; and I am still finding new meaning in it today . . . the meaning of my life.

The last words of the second reading, from the Gospel of Saint Luke: "those who yield a harvest through their perseverance" (8:15), bring to my mind a study Fr. Albert Derzelle asked me to make on patience in Scripture and the Fathers, especially on the Greek word *῾υπομονή*. It is found twice in Luke's Gospel, here (8:15) and in 21:19: "It is by your patience that you will save your lives (*in patientia vestra possidebitis animas vestras*)." The point of the parable of the sower is that a seed ought to be received, accepted, preserved and carefully guarded in the earth of the heart, just as the Word made flesh was in Mary's womb. This patience—constancy and perseverance—is proposed fifteen times by Saint Paul as the way to hope. The study was not unprofitable for me, seeing that half of life consists in things which one must undergo.

These two texts take on new meaning for me today as I call them to mind during this Eucharistic celebration, because salvation is now closer than on the day of my profession. "Night is almost over, it will be daylight soon . . ." (Rm 13:11).

On the card commemorating my solemn profession I wrote the last verse of Ps. 138:8: "Do not abandon the work of your hands," which echoes the formula in the rite of profession "May he who has begun these things in you bring them to accomplishment." This psalm is also one of gratitude: "I thank you, my God, with all my heart . . . the Lord will do everything for me!" (Ps. 138:1 & 8) . . . As for the two musical pieces, the one at the Offertory was sung at my solemn profession, and the *O quanta vis* . . . "O how great the power of love" was the antiphon of the Magnificat at Vespers on the feast of the Visitation, July 2. At the organ, Ghislain will play *Jesu, Joy of man's desiring*, in which John Sebastian Bach expressed so beautifully the peaceful joy of Christian hope, a fruit of this ardent patience which does not fail us. Once again, thank you, my brothers, for wanting to share these memories with me.

This homily was followed by a bidding prayer composed by Fr. Charles:

1. My gratitude to my parents, and first of all to my mother who taught me everything until I was eight years old—especially the catechism—and to whom I owe my vocation.

2. My gratitude to my college, to the Boy Scouts, to my comrades in my regiment during the war, to those who have helped me by their friendship.

3. My gratitude to my four abbots—since a monk ought to count on his abbot for everything—and especially to the one who during the twenty years of my afflicting illness showed me great kindness, often wrapped in humor.

> 4. My gratitude to my community and especially, among those who are not here today, to two true Scourmont monks even though each one was so different from the other: Fr. Thomas Litt, who taught me to reflect, and Brother Theophilus Darche, who taught me the art of suffering.
>
> 5. My gratitude to all those, present or absent, who have not been lacking in mercy toward me. May they know that I am thankful, and that I am aware of my debt to them.

One person who was not present on this special day but was much in Fr. Charles' thoughts, was his former novice master, Fr. Albert Derzelle, who had played such an important role in his life. During Fr. Albert's years as chaplain at the Clarté-Dieu, in Zaïre, he had become progressively incapacitated by a painful tropical disease. He died on Easter morning, 1993, after receiving the Eucharist.

Because Abbot Gerard was at Caldey for the regular visitation, the community did not have the usual Jubilee party for Fr. Charles that evening. Instead it was scheduled for the end of the month. As it happened, that very day King Baudouin, the Belgian people's beloved sovereign, died unexpectedly in Spain. The monks were grief-stricken, so Fr. Charles asked the community to cancel the get-together.

Chants de mémoire avant le jour **(Memory's songs before the dawn)**

There were, however, other occasions to celebrate his Jubilee. Besides visits from his family and some of his old friends from Boy Scout days, there was another very special celebration: a gathering with a group of poets, including the president of the Wallon Writers and the secretary of the Christian Writers. They came one afternoon with armfuls of flowers and met with Fr. Charles in Scourmont's guesthouse library to read and discuss poetry, some of it set to music. He was profoundly moved by their affection, esteem and friendship. Afterwards he wrote: "Not a bit of temptation of vanity, because as another poet said to me it comes from elsewhere . . ." (8.4.93).

To each person present at that gathering Fr. Charles offered a copy of his *Chants de mémoire avant le jour,* which had been published by Scourmont to coincide with his Jubilee. This collection of ten *Chants* was composed over a period of several years. He felt that they were a kind of retrospective view of his life, not in an anecdotic way, but rather as a continuous melody. Fr. Charles once said that he could remember the occasion on which he had written each of his poems, and this was true of the *Chants* as well as of his shorter poems. For example, the first one was begun in the train station at Nancy and finished at the Abbey of Ubexy; the seventh came to him at Igny on a glorious August day, the ninth in Switzerland during a retreat with the nuns of Collombey . . . The fact that he did write these poems over such a long period of time indicates how constantly he was occupied with thoughts of the life to come and the idea of time as expectation of eternity. As we have already seen, from his early years in the monastic life eschatology dominated Fr. Charles' interior vision. As it happened, the *Chants* were published at almost the same time as an article of his which also had to do with eschatology: *Action et Contemplation, Temps et Éternité.*[1]

The value of Fr. Charles' *Chants*—34 pages—attracted the attention of people thirsting for life in the spirit and also of poets, for its profundity and impeccable alexandrine versification. The booklet's symbolic cover photo shows Scourmont's church steeple outlined against the sky. Directly following the title page, there is this simple dedication by Fr. Charles: "To my community, after 50 years of monastic life, 1943–1993." These few words say so much. Had he not been known to say that it is not easy for a sick man in community? Community life was not easy for a poet, either. Yet he realized all too well how much he owed to his brothers at Scourmont and expressed his gratitude by offering each one of them a copy of these poems which were so precious to him. Fr. Charles

1. "L'Action contemplative, le temps dans l'éternité, d'après Saint Bernard," *Collectanea* 54 (1992) 269–283. Trans. C. Heaney, ocso, and P. Carroll, ocso, "Contemplative Action: Time in Eternity" (*Cistercian Studies Quarterly* 28 (1993) 145–159.

also sent copies of his *Chants* to some of his friends, including Professor Adolph Gesché, of Louvain, who in reply quoted another poet: "The pride of man advancing under the weight of eternity . . . By poetic grace the spark of the divine lives forever in the human silex."[2] Dom Jean Leclercq also received a copy and in a beautiful letter to Fr. Charles, wrote: "We share the joy of happy senior monks who are awaiting the Day" (11.2.93).

After the poets' gathering at Scourmont, as a way of thanking the monk-poet for the joy of that memorable afternoon, Roger Foulon wrote the following lines to Fr. Charles:

> To Charles Dumont,
> Several of us were assembled to praise
> The word, the word which comes from one knows not where
> And which transforms in an instant
> The most simple truth into fire, into a play of mysteries.
> The trees became blue fire-balloons
> Carrying heavenward our dreams and our souls.
> We heard the birds singing of their love to the flowers,
> We grasped in the poem a joyful pace,
> A bit like the tread of a deer in the wood
> When he seeks his mate, moaning and weeping.
> All this moved hearts and features,
> Sometimes a tear welled up. And the reader,
> Breathless, paused a short instant
> Like God, after six long days of work
> Holding in his hand heaven, animals, earth,
> And even man, who was going to invent the word.[3]

Jean Lacroix, another poet who had participated in the gathering at Scourmont for Fr. Charles' Jubilee, wrote an article which later appeared in *Collectanea* under the title: *Charles Dumont et la poésie-contemplation*.[4]

2. Saint-John Perse, Address at the Nobel Prize Banquet (Stockholm: December 20, 1960).

3. Roger Foulon to Père Charles Dumont. July 18, 1993.

4. Jean Lacroix, "Charles Dumont et la poésie-contemplation," *Collectanea* 57 (1995) 99–104.

> I was convinced that (Saint Bernard) would have approved of the two-fold way of proceeding that Charles Dumont has followed for a long time: writing texts and in-depth studies on spirituality with the same existential intention as when he writes poetry. In his opening talk at the Days of Study on Aelred of Rievaulx . . . Charles Dumont said: "Opening a book means entering into direct communication with a spirit; it means more particularly communicating with the thoughts of his heart. Still more, it means assuming the responsibility to accomplish what is written."[5] . . . In Chant V, I read:
>
> For the life of the spirit is a task to finish
> In the measured time of this passage in the world,
> A time to explore the space of desire.
>
> It seems to me that these verses summarize a whole poetic experience, what I will call the *living lyricism* of Charles Dumont, this lyricism which comes at the same time from action and contemplation, from silence and the interior word, from friendship with human beings and love of God.[6]

Death of Dom Jean Leclercq and Fr. Edmond Mikkers

During the autumn of 1993 Fr. Charles lost two close friends, Dom Jean Leclercq and Fr. Edmund Mikkers, both of whom died quite suddenly. Fr. Charles was asked to write a notice on each of these eminent scholars who were also humble monks. His notice for Fr. Edmund appeared in *Cîteaux,* the historical journal he had edited for years. It began: "It is only because of my friendship for him (Fr. Edmund) that I have undertaken this task: it is a kind of admiring account of him as a person who was both a monk and author."[7] After Vatican II, Fr. Edmund and Fr. Charles had worked together during the first stages of renewal of the

5. *Saint Aelred de Rievaulx, Le Miroir de la Charité. Journées d'étude,* Scourmont, October 5–9, 1992. *Collectanea* 55 (1993-1 & 2). This quotation appears on p. 9.

6. Jean Lacroix, "Charles Dumont et la poésie-contemplation," 100–101.

7. C. Dumont, "Le Père Edmund Mikkers, historien de la spiritualité cistercienne," *Cîteaux* 45 (1994) 7–19.

Constitutions of the Order. Through this study Fr. Edmund perceived that the evolution taking place within the monastic life, as well as in the diverse developments in theology at that time, was tending toward a resurgence of profound unity between theory and practice, and was aiming in one way or another at the unity which characterized the monastic life in the great periods of its history.[8] In 1992, Fr. Edmund had attended the *Days of Study on the Mirror of Charity.* He and his friend Dom Guerric sat next to one another during the lectures, sharing their impressions.

It was in the *Bulletin of the A.I.M.* that Fr. Charles' notice for Dom Jean Leclercq appeared:

> The relationship of our deceased friend with our monastery dated from his childhood. When he was in college at Avesnes he was familiar with our monastery and dreamed of becoming a monk here. He had only to hop on his bicycle and cross the French-Belgian border and he was here . . . He knew some of the monks of our community very well, and was especially friendly with Fr. Anselme Dimier, an historian like himself. As for me, I owe to him that he urged me to study the Cistercian Fathers, just as he helped so many others by his contagious enthusiasm. On the last off-print he sent us, shortly before his death, he added these few words: "To Scourmont, to whom I owe so much."[9]

Among the writings of Dom Leclercq that Fr. Charles referred to in this notice was his book *Bernard de Clairvaux,*[10] in which the Benedictine monk had developed more clearly than ever before the important role Saint Bernard played in the early history of Cîteaux. His efforts to draw attention to Saint Bernard's influence had gone still further in a later article which "led to a sort of apotheosis. He had, in fact, told some of his friends that it was like a

8. Ibid., cf. p. 16.

9. C. Dumont, "Dom Leclercq et les Cisterciens," *Bulletin of the A.I.M.* 56 (1994) 30–37.

10. Dom Jean Leclercq, OSB, *Bernard de Clairvaux* (Paris: Desclée, 1989). Bibliothèque d'Histoire du Christianisme 19.

bomb!"[11] This later article, entitled *La 'paternité' de Saint Bernard et les débuts de l' Ordre cistercien,* appeared in the *Revue bénédictine* in 1993. After reading it, Fr. Charles had remarked: "It seems to me that in this question of the origin of Cîteaux, which is still difficult, these pages shed a new and decisive light."[12] As a matter of fact, he had been delighted when he had seen Dom Leclercq's remarks, because Fr. Charles' opinion concerning the importance of Saint Bernard's role in early Cîteaux coincided with what Dom Leclercq had written, even though he himself had never dared to affirm it in print. So in his notice in the *Bulletin of the A.I.M.* Fr. Charles stated: "In our times when religious are continuously reminded of (the necessity to follow) the spirit of their founders if they want to bring about real renewal of their institutions, Saint Bernard's eminent place in the Cistercian reform cannot be overestimated by those who live according to it today."[13]

A lady who had done secretarial work for Dom Leclercq, Madame Gregoir, was living in Bourlers not far from Scourmont. She had become blind, so that Dom Leclercq communicated with her by messages on cassettes. The last one he sent to her before his sudden death contained this passage:

> . . . so you, too, speak to me about Charles Dumont; you ask me if he is a poet. Yes, he writes poems; he is very remarkable. I didn't know it, but recently he sent me a collection of his poems which were published for his fiftieth anniversary of profession —poems in French, very beautiful. He still writes poems in rhyme, real poems which rhyme, and at the same time he is erudite and very refined, especially as regards Saint Aelred who was a twelfth-century Cistercian author. . . . He reads English perfectly and reads a lot; he

11. "Dom Jean had told me that it would have the effect of a bomb!" ("Il fallait qu'il fasse ce coup avant de mourir." Letter, 1.26.94.) See "Saint Bernard and the beginnings of the Cistercian Order," in *Cistercian Studies Quarterly* 29 (1994) 379–394, and the review on it by Pierre-André Burton, ocso, in the *Bulletin de Spiritualité Monastique des Collectanea* 58 (1996).

12. C. Dumont, "Dom Leclercq et les Cisterciens," 34.

13. Ibid.

> gives lots of lectures on contemporary authors . . . so he is very cultured. (August, 1993)

Fr. Charles had two articles to finish before leaving for Latin America, one on Waldef (Aelred's friend in King David's court) and one on Aelred's biographer Walter Daniel, both for the concluding volume of the *Dictionnaire de Spiritualité*. After putting the last touches on them, he remarked, "So you see, a monk of Scourmont comes at the end of the *Dictionnaire de Spiritualité*, while Dom Anselme Le Bail, smiling, looks at him from the first fascicule (*Aelred* and *Bernard*) sixty years ago" (6.30.94).

The Southern Cone

A few days after Easter, 1994, Fr. Charles left for Argentina. After his arrival at Buenos Aires he went first to the Cistercian nuns' monastery at Hinojo. On the way, driving across the pampas he was so taken by their resplendent beauty that he wrote a poem: *Sur la pampa*. After his lectures at Hinojo he continued on to the monks' monastery at Azul and then visited the Benedictine nuns at Cordoba, Argentina. Madre Candida, of this community, former directress of the monastic review *Cuadernos Monasticos*, had visited Scourmont in the early 1980s. Fr. Charles then had three days of rest before taking a flight over the cordillera to Chile, where two other Cistercian communities—the nuns of Quilvo and monks of Miraflores—are located, both relatively close to Santiago. Quilvo was a high-point on his journey because it was there that he conducted a dense but well-followed seminar attended by twenty-five young monks and nuns, including the five novices of Miraflores. The conferences, translated into Spanish by Sr. Gabriela, of Hinojo, were based on his synthesis-in-the-making of Saint Bernard's spiritual theology. The last evening of his stay at Quilvo the students held a fiesta with national dances. On this occasion, he was invested with the Argentinean poncho, *honoris causa*! It was while Fr. Charles was at Quilvo that his nephew Christian De Vos was ordained as a permanent deacon in Chicago. Fr. Charles phoned him on this very special day and the two shared the great joy of this grace.

The monk-lecturer's journey to the Cono Sur made a profound impression on him. What exactly made Fr. Charles feel the way he did? For one thing, in all the monasteries he could see great interest in knowing the Cistercian Fathers. He had the impression that the monks and nuns listened to him the way he had listened to Dom Anselme fifty years before (cf. 5.19.94). He also noticed in the communities an awareness of the need to set aside time for study in their daily life. And of course there was the exuberant and intense latin color. Still, in addition to all that, there was something else which he could not define, so that he felt he should wait a while before trying to express it. In the countries he had visited there exists a religious foundation which two centuries of so-called *Enlightenment* has snuffed out in our western civilizations.

It is fundamental that the monastic life implies continual conversion. Still, there are crucial experiences on this path for each monk and nun. In the case of the monk whose life and works are being traced in this book, his journey to Latin America was perceived by him as being one of these experiences, just as his major operation in 1983 had been. These two experiences, though ten years distant from one another, seemed to connive in leading him to make a decision not to travel anymore.

> This decision comes at the same time from a sort of conversion to a more simple life (Cistercian!) which I had the grace to receive after my return from Latin America, and also from my evident duty to remain in the novitiate . . . But the novices learn everything by themselves. This morning Brother J. asked me some questions about silence. He sees how crucial it is for seeking God. It is my duty and joy to be here in the novitiate. I am passing some pleasant and useful hours reading the *Mirror of Charity* with Br. P. and the treatise on *Spiritual Friendship* with Br. J. (7.8.94)

Several months after his return from this journey, he wrote:

> (Ten years ago) I underwent a serious operation which endangered my life. But contrary to what the doctors thought,

> I did not come through it living, but dead. Judging by all appearances and the guarantee of scientific tests I survived; but a bit like Lazarus, apparently alive. I realize that even more clearly today . . . It is a matter of conscience, where each person alone is judge: greater awareness of my state of survival (from being deep-frozen to thawed) . . . When I woke up this morning what a surprise I had at Vigils! It was my turn to read the Scripture passage: the beginning of chapter 3 of the *Letter to the Colossians:* "Let your thoughts be on heavenly things, not on the things that are on the earth, because you have died, and now the life you have is hidden with Christ in God" (Col 3:2-3) . . . According to appearances I am still alive, resuscitated with Christ of course—that goes without saying—, and therefore my real life, the one which is hidden with him, will appear only when he will return on the last day. I live this strange interim as a dead man alive or as a living man who has passed through death. What is henceforth important for me is to be more aware of this. It will necessarily change my way of looking at things and people. There will be another *intentionality,* as the phenomenologists say.[14]

About the same time he wrote, "It is a rather curious experience, but truly, I have a second life since '83" (7.8 & 10.4.94).

In October the novices and their novice master attended a celebration for religious on the occasion of the ninth centenary of the Cathedral of St. Martin at Tournai. Bishop Huard had asked them to speak about their experience in the monastic life. That autumn Fr. Charles was also asked to speak about another kind of experience. The surgeon who had operated on him in 1983 invited him to address the national association of persons who suffer from Crohn's disease. Why did the doctor ask this fragile monk to speak? It was his opinion that "I was invited because I have a bit of humour and that is a form of love, isn't it?" (10.4.94).

As for his synthesis on Saint Bernard, Fr. Charles had intended to write the final version as soon as he returned from

14. *Eclaircies*. Unpublished. (January 3, 1995) 1.

Latin America, but now he did not feel ready to work on it. His decision to live a more simple and contemplative life coincided with some hesitation about the approach he should use in his synthesis. "I have always lived (intellectually) in fear of professorial judgment, and now I am breathing freely. I want to write freely—as certain people have been asking me to do—like I write my poems" (7.29.94).

When he did feel he could resume work on the synthesis it was with this approach, and he had no regrets about having waited. The style changed, the language was more sober and he left out a number of unnecessary quotations. Still, as always, he could never be sure that some health problem might make him interrupt his work. At Clairefontaine for a bit of rest, he looked out over the Semois placidly flowing through the valley in front of the monastery and wrote a poem. The following are several lines from it:

L'Esprit sur l'eau	**The Spirit over the water**
Au fil des flots du fleuve, *Sans passé, sans futur,* *Une âme soudain neuve* *Retrouve un présent pur.*	As the river flows by Without a past, without a future A soul suddenly new Rediscovers purity in the present.
Sur la Semois de cendre, *Comme un immense oiseau* *Je vis l'Esprit descendre,* *Dieu marcher sur les eaux.*	On the ashen Semois Like an immense bird I saw the Spirit come down, God walking on the waters.
Et c'est vers moi qu'Il vient *En ce moment fugace:* *L'Infini vers le rien* *Dans un monde qui passe.*	And it is toward me that He comes At this fleeting moment: The Infinite toward nothingness In a world which passes.
Un éclair, un instant *Baigné de lumière* *Au fil des flots du temps . . .* *Ce fut là ma prière.*	A flash, an instant Bathed in light Following the waves of time . . . This was my prayer.[15]
	1994.

15. *Poèmes et Prières,* 106.

Not long after, on the train between Charleroi and Liege he wrote another poem, scribbled on the only piece of paper he had at hand at that moment: the back of his ticket![16]

Praying the Word of God

At this time, Fr. Charles was preparing several lectures to be given on March 25, 1995, at the Jesuit Faculty of Theology in Namur. The purpose of the gathering being to introduce lay people to *lectio divina,* his topic was *Praying the Word of God.* He employed quotations from sources as varied as Fathers of the Church, modern scholars, poets and contemporary monks (just as in his lectures on the Virgin Mary to the lay audience in Charleroi) in order to present a fundamentally monastic method and practice in an understandable and palatable way to persons living in a nonmonastic context.[17]

The first collection of articles: Sagesse Ardente

During the Days of Study on Aelred at Scourmont in 1992 Fr. Charles had been encouraged to have at least some of his writings published in book form. Now, three years later, the first of two volumes of his collected articles, entitled *Sagesse ardente* (*Ardent Wisdom*), *the Cistercian school of love in the Benedictine tradition,* had just come off the press.[18] His pleasure when he received it was all the greater because preparation of this book had taken longer than expected. He had chosen as leadoff article *Saint Aelred: The Balanced Life of the Monk.* There were two reasons for doing

16. "L'amour d'un instant," in *Poèmes et Prières* 108. About the same time a short text by Fr. Charles entitled "Les mains des Anges. Le réalisme spirituel de Saint Bernard" appeared in *La Revue Générale* (February, 1995).

17. These lectures were published under the title. "La lectio divina pour prier," *Collectanea* 59 (1997) 13–31. Trans. "Praying the Word of God" (Oxford: Fairacres, SLG Press, Convent of the Incarnation, 1999).

18. *Sagesse ardente. À l'école cistercienne de l'amour dans la tradition bénédictine.* Pain de Cîteaux. Troisième Série, 8 (Oka, Qc.: Abbaye Notre-Dame du Lac, 1995).

so: it was the first article he had published in *Collectanea,* and it dealt with the balance to be maintained between the active and contemplative life by alternation of corporal and spiritual occupations.[19] As we have seen, throughout the years Fr. Charles always considered this aspect of monastic life to be of primary importance. Underlying all the articles in this new volume was the question of how the Cistercians saw the *Rule of Saint Benedict* and put it into practice. Now that this first volume with its handsome cover photo of the Fontenay cloister had come out, he began to look forward to seeing the second!

Death of Fr. Maur

Fr. Maur, whose health had been declining gradually for some time, received the sacrament of the sick toward the end of April, 1995, and died on June 21.[20] Though the two monks were very different by character Fr. Maur had been almost like an elder brother to Fr. Charles, especially during his student days and the first years he taught theology. Fr. Maur: utterly dependable and always available for advice on studies or being of service. He had directed the formation of two generations of monks at Scourmont. Fr. Charles was very affected by the death of Fr. Maur. It was as though an era—his era—was disappearing, but he realized that he should be looking toward the future. And look to the future he did. By June he had almost completed the final text of the third Chapter of his synthesis on Saint Bernard. Once again, however, this work had to take second place to other demands, in this case summer classes in philosophy for two young monks, Br. David from Caldey and Br. Placid from Mokoto, who were temporarily at Scourmont.

19. First published as "L'équilibre humain de la vie cistercienne d'après le Bienheureux Aelred de Rievaulx," *Collectanea* 18 (1956) 177–189. Trans. "Saint Aelred: The Balanced Life of the Monk," *Monastic Studies* 1 (1963) 25–38.

20. Dom Guerric, for whom Fr. Maur had been Prior for many years, was not at Scourmont at the time. Since early 1994 he had been chaplain for the nuns of the Clarté-Dieu (Congo Republic).

> I have a little bit of regret about this interruption, but it won't be a bad thing to stop for a while. It seems to me that the most difficult part (of the synthesis) is finished: the anthropology and Christology. And of course I ought to reply to what I am asked to do by obedience. I am not displeased! As I take philosophy up again I see that it is the only subject which I have ever really loved, and for me, poetry is a part of philosophy. (6.29.95)

Fr. Charles was even rather excited about beginning this particular philosophy course, because Br. David had asked if they could explore the writings of Emmanuel Levinas together. "I have always dreamed of doing this," he wrote, "and now here I am plunged into it—*face au visage!* It seems to me that my work on Saint Bernard will profit from this, too, because most often this face which attracts me is the face of Christ which was not unknown to him" (6.20.95). At the same time Fr. Charles was giving a course on Cistercian literature to Br. Pierre-André, and later in the summer there was a course on Dom Anselme Le Bail's *Twelve spiritual principles of the Rule* for a sister, from Hinojo, who was spending some time at Scourmont before beginning her studies at Louvain-la-Neuve.

On the feast of Saints Peter and Paul it was Fr. Charles' turn to give the homily at the Eucharist. Coming as it did just a few weeks after Fr. Maur's death, this homily is strongly marked by the thought of death. Saint Peter and Saint Paul did not teach us how to fish or make tents, nor to read Plato or Aristotle, he said, but how to live, which is the greatest thing of all. But to live, and live well takes on a different meaning in the face of death. Our real life is elsewhere; we are not of this world. Fr. Charles wove these thoughts together with references to both Levinas and Saint Bernard's *First Sermon on Sts Peter and Paul* because both the saint and the philosopher saw death as an opening on the infinite, on the absolute otherness (*altérité*), on God:

> What we can say about life before death . . . has no common denominator with the infinite over and above death,

> which is our true personal existence. Learning to live means not only learning to die but to approach death like a harbor where life's journey ends and a door opens on something else, on what we have always sought for, dreamed of, desired and loved among the beings and things of this world: limitless Being, eternal existence . . . The life of a monk is a sprint toward this infinity of God. The whole effort of the spiritual life comes down to living in the present with wisdom, reflecting on our past with sorrow in our soul, and preparing our future with patience and perseverance . . . Such unification of time already gives it an aura of eternity . . . "If you have some share in the sufferings of Christ, be glad, because you will enjoy a much greater gladness when his glory is revealed" (1 P 4:13). And as Saint Paul affirmed: "All I want is to know Christ and the power of his resurrection, and to share his sufferings by reproducing the pattern of his death" (Ph 3:10-11). Is this not the same Pascal Mystery which we are going to participate in now, in memory of the death and resurrection of Jesus Christ and of his two disciples who died amidst the sufferings of martydom?[21]

In late September, when Fr. Charles' birthday came around he celebrated it by writing a poem. "It came very easily, as if I had had all this time to prepare its birth." Without transcribing the whole poem here, the last three strophes will show how he saw God's action in his own life, and his constant occupation with the life to come:

Un Soir d'automne	**An autumn evening**
Comme un beau soir d'automne *Fruit mûr, ma vie est là.* *Complète, et je m'étonne* *D'un sourire un peu las.*	Like a lovely autumn evening Ripened fruit, my life is there Complete, and I astonish myself With a slightly weary smile.

. . . . . .

21. C. Dumont, "Homily for the Feast of Saints Peter and Paul," June 29, 1995, Scourmont.

J'attends calme en silence	I wait, calm, in silence
Que Dieu me dise : 'Viens !'	For God to say to me: 'Come!'
En attendant je pense,	And while I wait I think,
J'aime et me je souviens.	I love and I remember.
Toi qui connais ma vie	You who know my life
Du matin jusqu'au soir	From morning until evening
Toi, Seigneur, je t'en prie	You, Lord, I pray you
Garde-nous notre espoir.	Keep safe our hope.[22]

This same preoccupation with the life to come came up later in an interview with Fr. Charles which appeared in the Tournai diocesan newsletter under the title: *Living today as someone already risen.* This interview is quoted at length here:

> **C. D.** I live the resurrection already. The third chapter of the *Epistle to the Colossians* is perfectly clear on this point. To arrive at the resurrection, a person must have a deep knowledge of Christ by being united to him in his suffering. That means that by participating in Christ's sufferings I prepare for the resurrection. This makes all the difference. It gives meaning to my human sufferings, to my life and to my death. . . . (Many people) do not realize that there is Someone who is waiting for us . . . (Christians) suffer in life like everyone else. The only difference is that, by God's grace, there is an opening in the ceiling . . . Believing in the resurrection is first of all an interior experience. I am not more comfortable with myself because of it. The great mystics are the first to say so. Still, it is true that someone who believes in the resurrection can enjoy a certain interior peace. Nothing more. I myself have personally suffered a lot physically and socially. I have known distress. Yet, in the midst of trials, I have never lost the certainty of faith. . . . Believing in the resurrection is my whole life . . . but to live we must accept the reality of night.[23]

22. C. Dumont, "Un soir d'automne," *Prière et Poèmes,* 111.

23. *Vivre en ressuscité aujourd'hui,* interview with Frédéric Blondeau in *Paraboles, Revue diocésaine de Tournai 7,* March 1996, 4–5.

Fr. Charles resumed his work on the fourth chapter of the Bernardine synthesis, but had difficulty advancing in it. There had been a regular visitation at Scourmont which had remained open and the situation was not very comfortable for the monks. After Christmas he was not well at all, and when his doctor recommended that he go away for awhile Dom Gérard sent him to Caldey for ten days. He needed to regain his energy because in February he was scheduled to give another lecture to the students of the Institute of Theological Studies at Saint Michel College in Brussels.

This time the title of his talk at Saint Michel was *The spontaneity of religious obedience. Its phenomenological perspectives and Christological openness.* "I began by saying that I entered Saint Michel in 1926 to learn how to obey" (2.2.96). As to the development of his subject, for him the basic question was a human being's freedom before God. He told the young theologians that "true freedom, instead of being characterized by an attitude of defiance toward obedience and a claim to the right to be a free thinker, should find its full and peaceful flowering in obedience."[24] Supporting his remarks by quotations from such thinkers as Saint Bernard, Camus, Gabriel Marcel, Claudel and Levinas, Fr. Charles said that when we obey we act in a responsible way because we show our dependence on infinite freedom. The reason that we have free choice or will is that it may be saved by grace. Afterwards, he commented that the sixty students were a "perfect audience" and that he was pleased with the excellent questions they had asked after the lecture.

That same week Dom Gerard resigned as abbot of Scourmont, and for the time being no superior was appointed. As for Fr. Charles' health, all year long he had his ups and downs while he worked on Chapters Four and Five of the Bernardine synthesis. On the feast of the Assumption Fr. Corneille, one of the remaining monks formed by Dom Anselme Le Bail, died. Fr. Charles was deeply affected by his death, coming as it did so

24. C. Dumont, "La spontanéité responsable de l'obéissance religieuse," *Collectanea* 59 (1997) 107–117.

soon after Fr. Maur's. Fr. Corneille had been another co-disciple of Saint Bernard, having studied his works for years.

The 1996 General Chapter took place near Rome in October. As it happened the second volume of Fr. Charles' collected articles: *Une éducation du Coeur,* had come off the press just in time for copies to be given to some of the abbots and abbesses during the Chapter. This book, composed of articles on Saint Bernard and Saint Aelred of Rievaulx,[25] was welcomed by readers just as *Sagesse ardente* had been. Among the letters Fr. Charles received following its publication was one from a monk who had recently been appointed master of novices in his monastery. He expressed his appreciation as follows:

> I like very much the way you constantly link our tradition to what we are living today. In all these articles our Fathers are *living,* living for us, who are monks on the threshold of the third millennium. Yes, I was very happy to find that you are not an "archaeologist" or "a scholar," but a man of experience, experience which is like a path leading us to God by the community, the *Rule of Saint Benedict* and our Cistercian Fathers . . . I myself would like to be renewed in the spirit of our tradition and I would like to give to the novices entrusted to me this taste, this ardent love which is in you and which you have no doubt drawn from the heart of this *sagesse ardente* which is the school of charity. (6.4.97)

This kind of feedback encouraged Fr. Charles to persevere in his work on Saint Bernard.

Au Chemin de la Paix

All winter long Fr. Charles' attention was centered on this Bernardine synthesis, so that by spring he could write to a friend: "I put the final touches on my book several days ago, March 17

25. *Une éducation du cœur*. Pain de Cîteaux, Troisième Série, 10 (Oka: Éditions Abbaye Notre-Dame du Lac, 1996).

(St. Patrick's Day) at 5 p.m. I have a feeling of liberation—and also of being glad that I have been able to do it. 336 typed pages and 650 notes." The final choice of a title was: *Au chemin de la Paix. La sagesse cistercienne selon Saint Bernard.* Fr. Charles dedicated his new work "to all those in the Order who had helped him, and to all those who would read the book which was begun at Chambarand in 1978—twenty years before!" (2.2.97).

Meanwhile, at Scourmont the former Abbot General Dom Ambrose Southey had been appointed superior ad nutum and the community was getting back to normal. Dom Ambrose knew the monks well. Long before his visits to the abbey as Abbot General, when he was a student in Rome he had passed some of his vacation time at Scourmont. He reminisced with Fr. Charles about those days, recalling among other things that it was Fr. Charles who had given him his first French lessons in 1952 . . . over afternoon tea! Dom Ambrose took over the novitiate, which greatly relieved Fr. Charles.

The Contemplative Prayers

With his book on Saint Bernard at the publishers Fr. Charles could turn to other things. Some words of Pope John Paul II in an address to religious in Paris had captured his attention particularly:

> Your personal itinerary should be like an original re-edition of the famous poem of the *Song of Songs* . . . There one finds a profound theology of conversion which takes into account at the same time the power of God's grace and the human being's cooperation with it, the collective point of view finding an echo quite naturally in the personal situation of each person. (5.31.80)

Moved by these words of the Pope, Fr. Charles decided to make his own commentary on the *Song of Songs,* in the form of brief poetic prayers. As it turned out these prayers on the first thirteen verses of the first Chapter of the *Song* were composed over quite a long period of time. They were also different from anything else he had previously written. Some time afterward some of them appeared anonymously in the periodical *Vie Consacrée*.[26] Later on Fr. Charles continued his meditations on the *Song of Songs* with a second series of prayers. The fact that he wrote them over a long period of time leads us to suppose that he ruminated the sacred text over and over again before composing each one of what we might call these "prose-poems."

After Easter, 1997, for the first time since he had resolved not to travel anymore Fr. Charles made an exception and accepted to give a few lectures at Echourgnac, Le Rivet and Bonneval. His intention in giving these talks was very clear in his mind:

> I will speak about the spirit of the Founders and try to situate Cistercian spiritual literature in relationship to this spirit. Interest in historical research risks limiting the reform to archaeology and folklore, whereas it is incomprehensible if we do not take into account the upsurge of mystical evangelism at its origin. Saint Bernard is the soul of the reform and the master of the *schola Christi sub magisterio Spiritus Sancti* (4.5.97).

Yes, this was what he wanted to get across: the bond between the Cistercian Fathers' writings—especially Saint Bernard's—and the growth of the Order of Cîteaux, as has been mentioned previously. He returned from the south of France pleased with his visit to these communities, but still very tired. Dom Ambrose, seeing that some rest elsewhere would help Fr. Charles to regain his strength, arranged for him to go to Clairefontaine for a month. At the beginning of August he drove him to the monastery overlooking the Semois and entrusted him to the good care of the nuns.

26. "Prières contemplatives, par un moine disciple de Saint Bernard," *Vie Consacrée* 70, 3 mai-juin (1998): 187–193; 70, 5 sept.-oct (1998): 320–323; 71, 2 mars-avril (1999): 125–132. Reprinted in *Poèmes et Prières,* 135–164.

The Clairefontaine Retreat

There was no resident chaplain at Clairefontaine at that time, so Fr. Charles had the chaplain's house completely to himself. The evening of his arrival, browsing in the well-furnished library, he selected several books to read during his stay there. But then he suddenly remembered that he had already decided to pass a long period each day meditating the Word of God, and to write something in a notebook each morning. His resolution to read Scripture alone was strengthened by the temptation the library presented. He quickly put the books back on the shelves and felt good about having made his decision. During the next four weeks, in spite of the fact that he was frequently ill, he experienced great happiness in the program he had set for himself.

What he wrote each morning was actually a continuation of his commentary on the *Song of Songs,* not in the form of prayers this time but cursive meditations on the Gospel of the day's liturgy. He often sat outside in the chaplain's pleasant little garden with his notebook on his knees, writing down his thoughts. When he was well enough, he attended the Divine Office. Also, he still had not written the Epilogue to *Au Chemin de la Paix* which the editors of *Pain de Cîteaux* were waiting for, so some of his time was spent composing these final pages. By the end of the month Fr. Charles was feeling quite a bit better. The last lines written in his notebook were these:

> Resolution at the end of my retreat at Clairefontaine:
> I have but one thought:
> Forgetting what is behind me,
> Straining ahead with all my being
> To know Him
> and the power of his resurrection,
> and to share his sufferings
> by conforming myself to his death.
> Philippians 3:13, 10

The experience of his retreat at Clairefontaine was far too important to Fr. Charles for him simply to put aside his meditation when he returned to Scourmont. In fact, it was only several months later, on January 24, 1998, that he wrote the last lines. The *Clairefontaine retreat* [27] was the fruit of many years of deepening interior life.

During this period of intense reflection and prayer the thought came to Fr. Charles' mind to write his spiritual memoirs. He felt that this could be profitable not only to himself but to others, too. When he spoke of this to his superior, Dom Ambrose agreed and encouraged him to undertake this work. Other work was also cut out for him that autumn.

Louvain-la-Neuve

While Fr. Charles was progressing with his reflections on the *Song of Songs* he was also mentally preparing a very special lecture. His friend Professor Adolphe Gesché, dean of the faculty of theology at Louvain-la-Neuve, was organizing a colloquium to be held in late October on the subject: *Dieu à l'épreuve de notre cri (God, deaf to our cry),* and had asked Fr. Charles to give one of the talks.

The announcement for this colloquium explains its purpose:

> This meeting treats of the question of Job which is a question for all epochs and places: What becomes of the God who remains silent in face of our cry? It is a question that is radically up to date fifty years after Auschwitz, two thousand years after Jesus' cry on the cross; a question which rises from here and elsewhere, the cry of so many Holy Innocents. During the last twenty centuries, has the God of Gethsemani and the cross really been taken into consideration in theological thought? Does the crisis of modernity which brutally rediscovers the reality of evil and death not lead us to consider this God of the cross as the only one who is credible and can be thought of? It is in the manifestation of weakness as strength that God's truth reveals itself on the

27. Unpublished.

> cross. Does that not imply a logic of paradox which refuses to be illogical but claims its own logic?[28]

Fr. Charles had finished preparing his talk on this theme when he was asked to change his title to: *Man put to the test by God's silence (L'homme à l'épreuve du silence de Dieu).* He quickly recognized that it was fundamentally the same trial, but seen from the opposite side. The main thrust of his paper is that it is in times of trial that the human being and God meet in the most authentic way, because what is involved particularly at such times is our relationship with God, that is to say, our freedom and love.

> God's silence should be seen in this relationship made of word and silence—because our God is a God who speaks. Still, his word always calls us to go beyond ourselves and can seem to be his refusal to reply. In this case God's apparent silence is a chance for us to find the Word or the Silence of a loving and free subject who, over and beyond what we ask for, reaches the most true and profound desire and aspiration of our whole being. This relationship is love. God is love and his word and his silence cannot be other than expressions of it. *God is love.* (p. 2)

He explained that the Christian is someone who has willingly committed his or her freedom to the God of Jesus Christ in a covenant relationship. At the same time there is a continual temptation to take that freedom back. It is necessary to strive to clarify and fortify one's faith so that times of trial may become occasions for going beyond self. During his lecture Fr. Charles made reference to St. Bernard and Gabriel Marcel, as one could expect, but toward the end of the paper he also quoted Saint Theresa of Lisieux and the *Journal* of Etty Hillesum, the young Holocaust victim from Amsterdam whose writings had recently been published.[29]

28. The conferences given at this Colloquium were published in the volume *Dieu à l'épreuve de notre cri,* edited by Adolphe Gesché and Paul Scholas (Paris: Cerf / Université Catholique de Louvain, 1999).

29. Etty Hillesum, *An interrupted life* and *Letters from Westerbork. The Diaries 1941–1943* (New York: Henry Holt & Co., 1996) 376.

Fr. Charles felt that preparing this talk had been very important for him personally. On October 26, several days before the colloquium, he wrote:

> The conference which I am going to give at Louvain next Wednesday is finished. This morning I wrote the last page. As happens whenever I finish an article, a feeling of great relief came over me; but this time it was because of the theme being studied and the way I approached it, and also because I have been absorbed by this study for almost a whole year. I have the impression that in a way it is the culmination of my whole life. Not because I am invited to the University, where I have never set foot, but because I feel as though it is my entire intellectual and moral experience which I am confiding in these twenty pages of reflection on my life. Everything I say there is obviously over and above what I have attained, but if I have been able to write it simply and unhesitatingly, it is after all because I have always been convinced of it and have always tended toward it, in spite of so much weakness and so many faults.[30]

Publication of "Au Chemin de la Paix"

About the time when Fr. Charles was writing his reflections on the *Song of Songs*, the proofs of *Au Chemin de la Paix* arrived. After reading them through and returning them to the editor he wrote: "*Nunc dimittis servum tuum in viam pacis*. Today I sent off the proofs and sang these words with conviction and great joy" (2.9.98). One can easily understand why. This work, so painstakingly prepared over a long period of time, rethought and reworked again and again, step by step, was truly the work of a lifetime. As it happened, *Au Chemin de la Paix* came off the press in May of the Ninth Centenary of the Foundation of Cîteaux.[31] It was a happy day for Fr. Charles when he finally held

30. Unpublished notes.

31. *Au chemin de la Paix,* Pain de Cîteaux, 3e Série 13 (Oka, Qc: Abbaye N.-D. du Lac, 1998). Trans. E. Connor, ocso, *Pathway of Peace. Cistercian Wisdom according*

this book in his hands, and perhaps a compensation for having been unable to attend the celebration which had taken place at Cîteaux on March 21.

After the publication of his book it was not long before letters from readers began to arrive. One which particularly touched him came from a Cistercian of a community where he had lectured several times and given a retreat. The following lines are taken from this letter:

> It is to obey to a need of my heart that I express my thanks to you for this book on Saint Bernard. I should say rather THE book on Saint Bernard, because I believe that it is a 'landmark' and that from now on a number of publications on Saint Bernard will be inadequate and obsolete. Quite a few texts which are already familiar to me now appear in a new light, and I see them in relationship to my own life. Is this not THE way to read . . . ? And you are present at this 'meeting' . . . This is my way of telling you how very grateful I am to you. . . .

A review by the Jesuit H. Jacobs shows that Fr. Charles' new book was not only for Cistercians:

> This synthesis of Cistercian wisdom is profoundly expressive of the Abbot of Clairvaux's work, to which there are innumerable references. In dialogue with a great number of authors, this work seems to us to be unique in its type by its vast overview and its rich analyses. Saint Bernard's teaching is proposed to us here as a profound way of seeking God where grace and freedom meet and unite. It is a work of art rather than of erudition, as the author says when speaking of his study. Perhaps, but if the latter sort of works grow old quickly, his book enlightens and refreshes us by the youthfulness of its marvels.[32]

---

to Saint Bernard. Cistercian Studies Series 187 (Kalamazoo: Cistercian Publications, 1999). A translation in Italian appeared in 2000, and one in Spanish in 2002.

32. H. Jacobs, SJ. Review of *Au chemin de la paix. La sagesse cistercienne selon Saint Bernard, Vie Consacrée* 73 (2001) 61–62.

A new abbot at Scourmont: Dom Armand Veilleux

Dom Ambrose remained in charge as superior until September, 1998. At that time he asked to be replaced because of his age. Soon after, Dom Armand Veilleux was appointed superior *ad nutum* and after several months was elected Abbot of Scourmont in May, 1999. Dom Ambrose stayed on for a while at the abbey as novice master. That autumn of 1998, Fr. Charles' cousin Georges died. The two had always remained very close friends, united not only by family ties but especially by their priestly lives even though they saw one another rarely and Georges was so far away. He had passed his entire priestly life in Jordan, as a parish priest and principal of the Catholic school at Aqaba.[33]

About this same time Fr. Charles was having frequent attacks of tachycardia. His doctor recommended a new type of operation which proved to be both successful and painless. "I am prudent but cured of my attacks . . . It was my *tenth* operation and the best! Oh, progress! My health is good now and I aspire only to solitude" (12.8.98).

Thomas Merton Revisited

When Fr. Charles opened his mail one day he found a letter from Brother Patrick Hart asking him to write an article-review on the *Thomas Merton Journals.* How could he do otherwise than to accept, when it was a question of the *Journals* of his departed friend? Just recently he had written to another friend, "When I read Thomas Merton's *Journals* I often have the impression that he was writing them for both of us. How much suffering and joy there are for people who become monks in spite of so many problems, the principal ones being themselves." Switching to another subject, he continued, "I am meditating on the *Apocalypse,* on the mystery of our life (so small) in this cosmological,

33. In spring, 2002, Fr. Charles had a visit from a young woman studying at Louvain who was writing a thesis on Fr. Georges Dumont's pastoral ministry in Lebanon. Fr. Charles called this interview an "extraordinary experience."

ultimate, eschatological battle. Just to be there among the 144,000 before the Lamb is enough . . . shaping history. Merton was one of them when he wrote *The Seven-Storey Mountain*" (12.8.98).

Fr. Charles waded through the thick volumes, one after the other. As he went on, his conviction that Merton was a prophet became stronger. After several weeks he wrote: "I have almost finished the *Journals*—what an experience this is for me!—of sadness because of so much useless suffering, but also of joy because of this courageous and contemplative life of a man of such great human value" (2.1.99). While reading the fifth volume Fr. Charles was surprised to come upon an entry where his name was mentioned: "Father Chrysogonus is just back from Europe. He had a lot to say. Some good stories about Père Charles Dumont, my friend, editor of *Collectanea*"[34] Then when he reached the sixth volume he came upon the notes Merton had jotted down after Fr. Charles' visit to the hermitage. He approached the passage with curiosity and even eagerness because for years he had wondered what Merton had thought about him and that visit. One can imagine how crestfallen he must have felt when he read: "Père Charles speaks very softly with a Belgian accent and I can hardly distinguish what he is saying."[35] It was at such moments that Fr. Charles' keen sense of humor came in handy. After he had completely finished reading the *Journals* he still had not discovered the approach he wanted to use in his review article, so he contacted several monks who had lived with Merton at Gethsemani and had known him well. Even so, he needed more time to reflect on Merton the monk who was also a master writer, so he began to read through the entire *Journals* a second time. It was during this period that he also began to read the poetry of Czeslaw Milosz with whom he discovered greater affinity than with any other poet.

34. Thomas Merton. *Journals. Dancing in the Water of Life.* Volume 5. Ed. Robert E. Daggy (San Francisco: Harper, 1997) 299.

35. Thomas Merton. *Journals. Learning to Love.* Volume 6 (San Francisco: Harper, 1997) 35.

Several months later Fr. Charles received a beautiful letter from Fr. Francis Acharya of Kurisumala. The main reasons for this letter were to tell Fr. Charles how happy he had been to receive a copy of *Au Chemin de la Paix* and to thank him for sharing his community's joy about Kurisumala being incorporated in the Order. These two monks who had been fledglings under Dom Anselme Le Bail had been led by grace on very different paths. Now in their mature years each was reaping the harvest sown and cultivated during so many years, and with such care and labor. Fr. Francis' letter is quoted textually here:

Kurisumala Ashram, Kerala
Le 25 juin 1999

Very dear Fr. Charles,

What great joy, profound joy, when I received your letter of June 10: your impressions after looking through the commemorative album—texts and photos—of our incorporation in the Order; joy about these memories of Dom Anselme . . . and joy for your reflections on our fraternal union beyond time and space. . . . I often speak about you to the novices or the community to strengthen them in their vocation by the example of yours. When you came to Scourmont from school, without any diploma and in the midst of the turmoil of World War II, you shot up and grew in the monastic soil of Scourmont like a solidly-rooted plant, in spite of your physical fragility, bearing fruits that no one would have expected. What can be said of this growth except that it is the work of grace? What can be said of your works except that they are fruits of the Spirit, such as those Saint Paul refers to in *Galatians* 5:22? It is He who planted us on our mountain, who has helped us sink our roots here during the last forty years and, at a time when I myself—after vain efforts during the first ten years—thought no more about binding us to Scourmont, led the community to express that desire. We were received this time like the prodigal son in the parable by all those who came looking for us, and by the General Chapter who clothed us with the most beautiful robe and nourished us with the marrow of its traditions brought to light so very well during the last half of this century. You probably do not expect an answer, but I cannot leave your letter without an echo—even though a very weak one. I want to tell you once more how dear your affection is to me. It is a joy for me to feel that you are so alive in your so fragile body. A joy also to read your poems which seem to flow like living water from your trials and joys. I hope you are keeping a collection of them.

I embrace you with joy and great affection,

Fr. Francis.

Fr. Francis' sentiments were matched by Fr. Charles' joy when he received this letter of true and profound monastic friendship. Is this not the kind of friendship which St. Aelred wrote about?

After great joy, great trials

While conversing with his good friend Bishop Jean Huard one July day at Scourmont, "expressing to him my ideas on the Church and the world," as he put it, Fr. Charles "saw in the bishop's eyes that something strange was happening" (7.19.99). Dom Armand saw it, too, and had Fr. Charles sent to the Chimay Clinic immediately. What had happened was either a thrombosis or a threat of thrombosis. Thanks to prompt care his condition was controlled and there were no after-effects. During the following months, however, Fr. Charles was plagued with other illnesses and was back in the Chimay Clinic twice: first around Christmas time with pneumonia, and in March with a dangerous contagious bacterial infection. These periods in the hospital were special times of solitude. "*Habitare secum*—the best friend!" he said, after his third hospitalization, realizing that "these weeks were a marvelous interior grace. I am still very weak but am coming back to life. I thought I was going to die, but *si adhuc sum necessarius* . . . In the long run, one realizes that everything is grace and that all one needs is God's mercy. Mercy within mercy within mercy . . ." (3.24.00), he wrote, quoting from Merton's *The Sign of Jonas*.

It was shortly after his return from the hospital that he learned of the death of his brother-in-law, Raymond DeVos.

Fifty years of Priesthood

May 18, 2000, marked the 50th anniversary of Fr. Charles' ordination to the priesthood. He wanted to spend that day at Soleilmont because, as he said, it was there that he had exercised his priestly ministry most, during the twenty years he had been chaplain for the sisters. It was a happy day for him and the community. As often happens joy is followed by sorrow, and so it was this time. Just one month later Dom Thomas Vilain, who was Dom Armand's Prior, died quite unexpectedly. Fr. Charles sorely missed Dom Thomas' affability and their conversations, because they had become good friends. Though unwell, he attended the funeral and even followed the procession to the cemetery. As time went by he was living more and more a life of a recluse, which however had nothing to do with idleness. Reading Saint John occupied him increasingly. After long years of study he was happy to be able to write more personal spiritual things, notably a series of meditations on the Farewell Discourse in Saint John's Gospel. He explained:

> Since I received the grace of a sort of conversion this year, due to my illness, I am reading Saint John as I have never read him before, as no one has ever read him, because this *lectio* has become personal, intimate, captivating, decisive. I pray in my quality of son. "My sheep listen to my voice. I know them and they follow me. I give them eternal life" (Jn 10:27). In the background is the knowledge I have acquired in a life of study, but it remains there and I *listen to his voice*. It is marvelous. I can remain for hours on one phrase or even on a word . . . This peace leaves in the background everything which could trouble me in this difficult life. (6.19.00)

One aspect of his reflection centered on the impression he had of seeing his life as a whole. This had already occupied him several years earlier, when he was at Poyo:

> While I was composing the following poem, I saw the difficulty of speaking about this impression of seeing one's life as a whole. A remark by Gabriel Marcel seems to me to correspond very well to my feelings, that is, to speak of my past as a whole means to adopt a hybrid attitude. It means contemplating what one has lived, without deciding to stop living it. So I wrote this poem in the line of thought which occupies me constantly and totally: eschatological hope, which was my whole spirituality when I was a young monk and which I had lost for all kinds of reasons. But what joy it is to rediscover this former fervor, to finish—that is to say, to begin—to live. Death, this birth . . . As I reflect on it, I believe that everything essential in my life is in my *Chants,* and then, in my *Considerations,* in my letters, and also a little in my articles. (11.2.93)

L'Attente	**Waiting**
Quel sera mon dernier soupir	Which sigh will be my last
Essoufflé de la grande épreuve:	Breathless from the great trial:
De désespoir ou de désir?	Of despair or desire?
De quel amour fera-t-il preuve?	What love will it prove?
À ce temps d'un soupir: la vie	In this time of a sigh: Life
Où est le début et la fin?	Where is its beginning and end?
L'éternel qui nous convie,	The eternal which invites us,
Ai-je cessé d'en avoir faim?	Have I ceased to hunger for it?
J'ai traversé un flot d'instants	I have crossed a flood of instants
Chacun par son evanescence	Each by its fleetness
Espérait le dernier. J'attends	Hoped for the last. I await
Le port, la mort, cette naissance.	The port, death, this birth.[36]

Scourmont, 1993.

36. *Poèmes et Prières,* 104.

Visitors came to see him: poets, close friends, monks. It was in this life basically not unlike the hermitage life of his late friend Thomas Merton that he felt he had finally discovered in the maze of the *Journals* the source of unity between Merton the monk and Merton the writer. He felt that at last he could set about writing the review of the *Journals*.

7

THE MONK-POET AND POET-MONK

Everything is a symbol and passes,
Sea, heights, immensity,
Everything takes on meaning and disappears
I reach Reality.

C. D., *The interior Ascension*

Publication of "Poèmes et Prières"

One day Fr. Charles said he would like to see Dom Dieudonné Dufrasne, a monk of Clerlande and frequent visitor at Scourmont. With Fr. Charles' assistance Dom Dieudonné had just finished writing a book on Dom Anselme Le Bail.[1] For Fr. Charles, collaboration with his Benedictine friend had been both a pleasure and a token of filial gratitude toward his first abbot. It meant bringing to mind many memories of this great monk who had been the dominant influence in his entire monastic life. This particular day Fr. Charles had a special reason for wanting to see Dom Dieudonné. He wanted to entrust to him an important part of his own writings. "I bequeathed my 100 poems to Dom Dieudonné. I do not know what will become of them. As far as I am concerned they have helped me to live, to dream, to think and to remain free. I let them go like an apple tree drops the apples it has borne . . . Really, my whole life is in them" (1.26 & 2.18.00).

1. Dom Dieudonné Dufrasne, OSB, *Dom Anselme Le Bail, Un Moine, Un Abbé, Une Communauté* (Scourmont: 1999) Cahiers Scourmontois 1.

What became of them is that Dom Dieudonné edited them and they were published as *Cahier Scourmontois* 2, entitled *Poèmes et Prières* at Christmas time, 1999. In addition to his poems—including the previously published *Chants de Mémoire avant le Jour*—the volume contains Fr. Charles' first series of *Contemplative Prayers* on the *Song of Songs,* some of which had already appeared anonymously in *Vie Consacrée,* as has been mentioned.[2] Two Preface letters introduced the poems: one by Fr. Charles entrusting them to Dom Dieudonné, the other by Dom Dieudonné expressing his acceptance.

While waiting for the book to come out, Fr. Charles reflected on the place of poetry in his life: "The poet and the monk, the enigma remains for me; either-or, or neither, or one? . . . It is in my poems ultimately that I recognize myself best. When I see the first copy, it will be my dream as a fifteen-year old come true" (10.20. & 12.4.00). After the book's publication favorable reviews soon began to appear. The first was a review article by the editor of *Collectanea,* Fr. Bernard Joseph Samain, a monk of Orval. He, like others hitherto familiar only with Fr. Charles' work in the field of monastic studies, expressed his astonishment:

> Editing and translating Aelred, offering us a synthesis of Saint Bernard's spirituality, teaching Gabriel Marcel's philosophy, admiring the theology of Cardinal Newman, reviewing books on monastic spirituality for *Collectanea Cisterciensia,* or serving as an expert on the *Cistercian discipline or life* at meetings here or there, these are all well-known facets of Father Charles' activity. But there is a more secret space in this monk: his poetic side —or should I say his poetic "a-side"—which we are just beginning to know.[3]

Actually, in his review Fr. Bernard-Joseph dealt less with Fr. Charles' book than with the negative attitude toward poetry which prevailed in Trappist monasteries in the past, and he ex-

2. See Chapter 6, pp. 149–150.

3. Bernard Joseph Samain, OCSO, "Moine et Poète . . . À propos du recueil *Poèmes et Prières* du Père Charles Dumont, " *Collectanea* 63 (2001) 191–200.

pressed regret for the poems Fr. Charles had never been able to write because of this false type of ascesis. At Scourmont, however, no such attitude had ever existed. Dom Anselme Le Bail had not forbidden the young Brother Charles to write poetry, but had simply advised him to practice moderation in doing so, just as in everything else. Nowhere in Fr. Charles' writings or remarks is there any trace of frustration or bitterness about not having been able to practice this art more freely. "I don't think the discipline was an obstacle to my freedom, but there was the sheer fact that I lived in a very cold climate as regards that level of culture" (7.24.01). He was also aware of the perils which can threaten a poet. At the beginning of the original typewritten collection of his poems—which grew as the years went by—he had put this *Avertissement,* this warning by Kierkegaard, to be cautious: "What I have so often said: poetry is a dangerous gift for the poet and for others; instead of its being conversation in which one is committed, it risks turning into an aesthetic bonfire."[4]

In the Cistercian life long years of silent growth produce their own quality of fruit, and this seems quite evident in Fr. Charles' poetic work. As has been pointed out, he remembered exactly in what circumstances and when each poem was written, although he never reread his poems.

Shortly after his book appeared Fr. Charles was again interviewed by Frédéric Blondeau, one of the editors of *Paraboles* (diocese of Tournai). Part of this interview entitled: *La liberté d'un poète (A poet's freedom)* is reproduced here because the basic attitudes and dispositions of a poet—and of this particular poet—are so well articulated in it.

F. B. In your work, you make a clear distinction between poems and prayer, yet when we read your poems we have the impression that even if they are inspired by the little things in life they are already prayers which open out on what is beyond.

C. D. Actually, there is a mysterious kind of osmosis between poetry and prayer, but with appreciable differences. So when the

4. Søren Kierkegaard, *Journal,* 27.

poet speaks of God he does not meet him by doing so. The point of contact between poet and mystic is the infinite. Both seek the infinite. The difference is that the mystic knows it, but the poet does not necessarily know it. The mystic does not know God, but he is sure that he can love him and know him. Like him, the Christian poet knows that he is seeking the infinite. He believes that God exists; still, he does not reach this truth by poetry but by faith.

F. B. Is there a connection between your vocation as a poet and your monastic vocation?

C. D. No doubt. Before wanting to become a monk, I was a poet. And it was an awesome poet, Saint Francis, who fanned the flame of this desire in me. I think that poetry is the best way to express the **Mystery**. And it is not by hazard that Saint John of the Cross is the greatest mystic and best poet—at least as I see it. When I read his *Romances* I discovered what liturgical language should be: a poetical description of dogma. Poetic language is not enclosed in a type of logic: it liberates. It is par excellence the language of Revelation, of Scripture, of the contemplative, of faith. Unfortunately, the Church has partially broken away from this language. Our celebrations are terribly lacking in poetry. Today, in the liturgy, we are wordy. As for the poet, he communicates something else than ideas. He writes with all his being, his body, his flesh. Like the psalms, some of my songs are very sensual. This is important; otherwise they would not signify anything at all.

F. B. It is true, isn't it, that society today has broken with poetic language and considers it to be capricious and of little worth?

C. D. Actually, it is very harmful for a human being to be deprived in this way of an essential dimension of his or her being. I can see two ways of looking at poetry. There is poetry which is an art and at the same time a demanding technique which consists of putting words, images and symbols together. And then there is the poetry which everyone has within him or herself, in different proportions, like a second condition. I would define it as *dissatisfaction with the finite which every human being experiences.* The miracle of poetry is that it succeeds in describing this tension between fragility and eternity. It touches the heart. That is why it is meaningful only to those who love and know the suffering of passionate love which never fully attains the beloved. And it is because they reveal what is deepest within a human being that the poet, the artist and contemplative are universal.

F. B. In your opinion, what is the most important quality of a good poet?

C. D. The same as that of a good monk: to be true . . . real![5]

À toi qui lis ces vers	**To you who read these lines**
Je sais que mon poème *Oiseau captif, s'en prend* *À la vitre du temps* *Et se cogne à lui-même.*	I know that my poem, Captive bird, is caught on The window of time And strikes itself.
Plus sage est ma prière *Plus paisible et sans cri* *Dans les mains de l'Esprit* *Elle attend, elle espère.*	Wiser is my prayer More peaceful and with no cry In the Spirit's hands It waits, it hopes.
Dans les blancs et les marges *Tu sauras discerner* *Si mon Coeur est cerné* *Et quand il est au large.*	In the spaces and margins You will be able to see If my heart is cramped And when it is open wide.[6]

In a review, which appeared in *Vie Consacrée,* J. Burton, SJ, called Fr. Charles' book "an admirable atlas of the maps of time and the eternal, glowing with the light of Easter."[7] A professor friend of Fr. Charles began his comments to the author by a phrase written by Fr. Charles himself:

5 "La liberté d'un poète," interview with Frédéric Blondeau. *Paraboles,* Revue of the Diocese of Tournai.

6. *Poèmes et Prières,* 11.

7. J. Burton, SJ, *Vie Consacrée,* 4 (Juillet-Août, 2002) 275.

> "Do not sever words from the soul which thinks them. They would lose their life." Since the life of a monk is to seek God, it is also the pursuit of Truth, of Him who said *I am the Truth* (Jn 14:6). (Fr. Charles') initial act of faith no doubt determines the meaning and form of his texts, but especially and more fundamentally the form of his life . . . A poet is someone driven by desire to approach a horizon. Charles Dumont is a monk who lives in two worlds. His prayer and poetry are the bridge between the two.[8]

As always, Fr. Charles' mind was occupied with something else he was going to write. This time it was the review—article on the Merton *Journals*. He had been mulling them over in his mind for months as he reread them from beginning to end, and now he felt he could put his thoughts on paper. So he set about this task of head and heart, writing longhand because he was no longer strong enough to type or use a computer. As he advanced Fr. Charles had to come to grips with Merton's frustrations about the way the contemplative dimension of monastic life was being threatened by preoccupation with material concerns, his impatience with detailed usages and his differences of opinion with his abbot. All these things had rubbed against the grain of Merton's artistic and poetic nature, but nothing had been able to turn him aside from his desire for God and his longing for an ever deepening contemplative life. Had Fr. Charles also not suffered from the same sort of things in daily life in the monastery? His article is that of a contemplative poet writing compassionately about another contemplative poet.[9]

Merton had remarked in his *Journal* that Hannah Arendt's work *The Human Condition* was a "hinge on which one's whole thought can turn. A whole new aspect of action and contempla-

8. Unpublished.

9. C. Dumont, "La disparition prophétique de Thomas Merton," *Collectanea* 63 (2001) 332–351. Trans. "The Prophetic Disappearance of Thomas Merton," *Cistercian Studies Quarterly* 37 (2002) 373–392.

tion . . ." [10] Since everything which touched upon the dynamic action-contemplation interested Fr. Charles, he looked into this book. "It is a question of an analysis of the *vita activa* and its evolution from the classical period of the Greeks for whom the contemplative and political spheres could be one, but especially from the time of the Romans who stressed work and denatured it, giving it preference over the *vita contemplativa.* The problem is *there,* but without any visible remedy in our dominant technocracy" (4.17.02). Reading this book of Hannah Arendt led Fr. Charles to reread Plato's *Republic,* always in search of something else which would throw new light on this important question.

Concurrently he was reading a masterful work on Christ by Professor Gesché and more of Emmanuel Levinas, with whom he felt increasing affinity. One reason for this was that Levinas did not separate philosophy from moral life and religion. All this reading went on in his room. To make things easier for him, one of the monks had given him a very practical little bookcase on wheels. In the past it had belonged to Fr. Albert Derzelle, so that it was especially precious to him. From his window he could look out over the lawn, sky, flowers, shrubs, trees—especially the birch tree he had written a poem about years before. After Ascension Day he wrote, "The Risen Christ always arrives unexpectedly, but at my age I should expect him more seriously. I'm trying and am helped by my physical condition, in a comfortable armchair, looking endlessly into the heavens through a large window until he will come" (5.5.02). Shortly after writing these lines Fr. Charles saw his cardiologist, who told him that he had the heart of a young man! Even so, he remained unable to participate actively in the life of the community except for concelebrating at daily Mass and taking his meals in the refectory. As he put it, he was learning blessed and difficult solitude.

That summer Fr. Charles' nephew Christian and his wife Marnie came to visit him. The following poem which he wrote for

10. Thomas Merton, *A Search for Solitude.* Journal 1952–1960. Volume 3. Ed. Lawrence S. Cunningham (San Francisco: Harper, 1996) 389.

Marnie after this visit shows how the life to come was constantly in his thoughts, even in the pleasant company of his family.

Quand je serais bien mort *À la fin de ma vie* *Je prendrai essor* *L'âme sera ravie*	When I will really be dead At the end of my life I will take flight My soul will be snatched up.
Touchant Dieu sans effort *Toute soif assouvie* *Dans l'azur bordé d'or* *De bonheur éblouie.*	Touching God without effort All thirst slaked In the golden-edged blue Dazzled with happiness.
Présence douce et tendre *Il suffit de l'attendre* *Comme on attend le jour*	Sweet and tender presence To await it is enough Like one waits for daybreak
De là où je serai *Tout près du grand Amour* *Je vous appelerai.*	From there where I will be So near to great Love I will call you.

About that time Scourmont was updating its audio-visual program on the monastery. Dom Armand asked Fr. Charles to prepare a two-minute summary of Cistercian spirituality to read before the camera. The following is his text:

Cistercian Spirituality

By their solicitude to be true to the Gospel in their reform of the monastic life, the first Cistercians gave a special place to three themes: greater faithfulness to the spirit and letter of the *Rule of Saint Benedict*, stricter personal and communal solitude which foster contemplative prayer, and love of Christ poor and humble: the God who became man. It is this last one, the divine Incarnation, which Saint Bernard endeavored to develop, thereby giving a new sensitivity to all Christian spirituality: Christ approached humanity by love. This soon became the principal charism of the Cistercians' life, both interior and exterior. Application to reading and studying the Bible and their spiritual masters' commentaries on it, especially their homilies on that sacred song of love: the *Song of Songs,* made their teaching and life what they called a school of charity—even a *special* school of charity, or a school of the Holy Spirit. In this school, first of all and above all, one teaches and learns to obey God's first commandment, the source from which the others flow: "You shall love . . ." (Mt 22:37). There the monk or nun applies him or herself first of all to studying the psychology of love which for them is founded on freedom. Freedom is the most distinctive trait of the soul created in the image and resemblance of the Creator's infinite freedom. A human being's freedom is exercised especially in natural affectivity which by grace becomes charity or spiritual love.

Dom Anselme Le Bail, a former Abbot of Scourmont, was able to affirm that Saint Bernard wrote only one treatise on spirituality, that of the soul's relationship to God: love. But love of God cannot exist without humble love of self and love of one's neighbour. For Saint Aelred of Rievaulx, who spread Cistercian spirituality throughout England, these three loves go together and are interactive. In his *Mirror of Charity* Aelred showed how the three of them work together for the soul's peace with self, others and God. One form of charity became the subject of another tract by Aelred: *On Spiritual Friendship.* There he shows his deep knowledge of the human heart and also of God's heart. This Cistercian spirituality, even if it dates from nine-hundred-years ago, has a good chance of remaining alive and attractive because of what is essential in it. Because God is love and we are, too.

Death of Father Robert and Bishop Huard

In October both Fr. Robert Pourtoit—who had been occupied with the financial administration of Scourmont for years—and Fr. Charles' dear friend Bishop Jean Huard died. Fr. Robert had been at Caldey at the same time as Fr. Charles when they were still young monks, and it was there that he had known him best. It was no doubt at Caldey that Fr. Robert became acquainted with the works of Cardinal Newman which he continued to study for years.

October also brought back memories of the First Trimester at Chimay. The year 2002 marked the thirtieth anniversary of this Patristic-Cistercian course which had made such a deep impression on all the participants. Ever faithful to his friendships, before Christmas Fr. Charles asked a nun at Chimay to search in the archives at N.-D. de la Paix for his last-day message to the departing students in 1972. She found it where Sr. Lutgarde, the archivist of yore, had carefully put it: "Rest, my soul, in your secret cellars, the three perfume rooms: love of self, love of God, love of others." These words were accompanied by a drawing by Fr. Charles representing three Cistercian vaulted cellars. He sent a copy of this memento to each of the 1972 students. The replies were gratifying. The nuns still had clear, living memories of that very special trimester and shared his sentiments entirely. After reading their letters, he wrote to one of them: "*On n'a pas fait mieux depuis*" ("Nothing better has been done since.") During that autumn or winter of 2002 two or three of the ex-students had an occasion to visit Scourmont and reminisce with Fr. Charles about those memorable months passed at Chimay.

During the winter Fr. Charles was occupied particularly with his ongoing meditation on the Lord's farewell discourses in Saint John's Gospel. Reading them made him think of how, when he was a young monk, he used to love to read Newman's sermons for feast days. He also had ample occasions for philosophic reflection, because a doctoral candidate at Louvain-la-Neuve who was writing a dissertation on Husserl came regularly to talk with him about phenomenology. This, of course, he found very stimulating. In another vein, he was writing more prayers on the *Song of Songs* and rewriting his memoirs. And there were visits, the most notable one being that of the Abbot General, Dom Bernardo Olivera, with whom he had the joy of a long conversation.

As for poetry, three years had gone by since Fr. Charles had written his last poem, saying that he would write no more. Then, in spite of his decision, another one came to him quite spontaneously. He entitled it: *L'épreuve de l'amour (The test of love)*. When one looks back over his earlier writings, one finds that certain thoughts expressed in this poem had come to his mind at different periods of his life and in various contexts. He said that his memoirs, the *Prayers on the Song of Songs* and this long poem all seemed to go together to express his whole life. Fr. Charles considered this poem to be his spiritual testament, as it were, a summing-up of years of reflection on the significance of his life as a man created by God and a monk destined to return to God.

At the time when Fr. Charles was composing this long poem he was obliged to rest quite a lot during the day and consequently slept rather poorly at night. In those silent hours, turning each line of this poem over in his mind he sometimes rose, took his pen in hand and changed a word or phrase. What better way could there be to conclude this book than to present this entire poem followed by Fr. Charles' commentary on it? In these lines it is as though he is walking on the road of life with the reader, pointing out the way as they go along.

The Test of Loving

La vie est à penser comme une épreuve *—Parcours à franchir en temps donné—* *Qu'il te faut bien accueillir sans preuve* *Pour aimer ce pourquoi tu es né.*	Life is to think of as a test —A road to travel in given time— That you must accept without proof To love this why you were born.
Si la route est grise et monotone *Prends alors ton plaisir à marcher* *Si ta paix, tout en allant, t'étonne* *Tu sauras le bonheur de chercher*	If the road is monotonous and gray Take pleasure then in walking; If your peace, as you go, amazes you You will know the happiness of seeking.

De chercher au plus profound qui soit
(Et c'est même en cela qu'est l'épreuve)
Celui seul plus toi-même que toi
Pour aimer lui en donner des preuves.

To seek in your deepest self
(And it is exactly that, the test)
Him alone more yourself than you
To love him by giving him proofs.

Or, il n'est d'autre preuve d'aimer
Que l'amour: "J'aime puisque j'aime;"
Ne feront qu'un, l'amant et l'aimé,
Qu'aspirés dans cet amour supreme.

Now, there is no other proof of loving
But love : "I love because I love;"
They will make but one, lover and loved,
Only when drawn into this love supreme.

L'amour reste à l'épreuve du temps
Le trouver, c'est le chercher sans cesse,
L'attendre, le saisir un instant,
S'en souvenir pour qu'il reparaisse.

Love bears the test of time:
To find it is to seek it unceasingly,
To wait for it, grasp it for an instant
To remember it, so it will reappear.

Parfois la vie est comme un sommeil
Peuplé de cauchemars ou de rêves:
Une nuit pour mûrir un réveil
Éternel, qui nous la rendra brève.

Sometimes life is like sleep
Peopled by nightmares or dreams:
A night to ripen an awakening
Eternal, which will make it seem to us brief.

L'épreuve est d'attendre infiniment
Que se révèle à tous ceux qui l'aiment
Cet amour qui attend ardemment
De les révéler tous à eux-mêmes.

The test is to wait infinitely
Until to all who love it is revealed
This love which ardently waits
To reveal them all to themselves.

Le désir est le bonheur d'attendre
Et la paix, d'être aimé et
d'aimer
Le feu doit rester feu sous la cendre,
Et patiemment te consumer.

Desire is the happiness of
waiting
And peace, to be loved and
loving.
The fire must remain fire under
the ashes
And patiently consume you.

Et quand viendra ta mort corporelle
Au bout de ce chemin
qui finit,
Que lui échappe une âme
immortelle
Et qu'elle aille aimer à l'infini!

And when your bodily death
will come
At the close of this road which
ends,
Let the immortal soul escape it
And go on to love infinitely!

Fr. Charles signed the above poem on January 6, 2003, adding: "in my sixtieth year of monastic life." It is a work born of Fr. Charles' desire

> to think a bit seriously and without projection, if possible, of my future personal life; nothing is impersonal. With this intention, I do not think that I can begin in a better way than to go back over this poem I have written—the last—, to think back over my existence from beginning to end. While writing this poem—my longest (except for my *Chants*)—I had the strange and beautiful sentiment of (invisibly) seeing come together those whom I have loved and who have loved me. At each verse, or almost, a memory came to my mind. Each one gave and re-gave me life. Each one was given to me by God with my life. Each one was willed by his love. And it is thus, as I can see by my faith and His grace, that it appears to me as a beautiful test, the kind I dreamed of when I was a child, an obstacle course, a

> dangerous leap, a beautiful adventure. I have not reached the end of the test, but I have a glimpse of the end and I am running toward it as if to my mother's arms. Is it not she whom I loved first?[11]

Fr. Charles wrote out what this poem signifies to him. His comments are transcribed here, in italics, on the following pages (176–187).

Fr. Charles' Commentary on the Poem "The Test of Loving"

The repetition of the title of the poem in the first verse signifies for me that love implies not only a test but that the test is one and the same thing as love, that it is identical to love and that "it is its life." This last formula, which has become banal and vulgar, nevertheless expresses the truth. It is in this testing where love continually rediscovers itself that the true life of the soul is found. "Life as a test" is a way of seeing it which led Gabriel Marcel to faith and Baptism after long years of reflection. If the whole of my life is in fact a test, it is not possible that it has been imposed upon me by myself, and if it has been given to me as such it must have a meaning. For the Christian believer, it follows that if the Creator is Love his creature can in no way be anything else. The test therefore is a test of love and it gives us the meaning of life, which we believe opens out into eternal life—that is to say the infinite—above all limits and any kind of conditioning resulting from time and space. The test of love is precisely the test of its finite state: waiting and hoping for the fullness of life. The last verse of the poem thus will cast us into this infinite which exceeds everything, because love is as strong as death.

The title of the poem (the title of a poem comes most often to a poet after the poem is finished) will become clear as the poem is being read, just as it slowly emerged while the poet was writing it. The reader will see the meaning of the term "test," which does not mean the "trials" which weigh a person down . . . As concerns love, it is Christian love and at the same time just simply love. If the two words: the test *and* loving *are joined together, it is in the sense that life unites them. The test therefore is life itself, in which love is born and matures. Subject to time simply by the*

11. Unpublished text.

course of existence, like all temporal life it knows its alternations and vicissitudes as well as the coming and going common to all changeable beings. This applies to all human love, whether its object is God, one's neighbor or oneself. Still, one never loses sight of the fact that it is a test and that consequently it has a meaning, an end, a goal and hope.

1 Life is to think of as a test
—A road to travel in given time—
That you must accept without proof
To love this why you were born.

Life can be thought of in many different ways, but in reality that is not so often how it is. It is not a question of philosophizing, of moralizing or of judging. It is a question of—while we go on living—being astonished that we can reflect on our life, think back over it in our memory and with surprise find ourselves on the way toward a plenitude: a kind of doubling of ourself and the self which we are always searching for, which is always further on. So the test is situated in this race forward that we become conscious of from time to time . . . "To remember oneself in fragments of dreams" (Chant 1, v.1).

Seen retrospectively, life—at least as concerns the part of it one has already lived—can therefore be thought of as being limited and even ephemeral in time and space. Its reality is nonetheless the only one which is concretely accessible to us and therefore the only one in which the eternal is graven.

The two lines that follow are simply the natural conclusion from this fact. All that thoughts can dream of, imagine or design reposes on this indubitable, irrecusable and inevitable fact of having been born, that is, created. Interpretations vary and can even change from one moment to another, but the original fact remains—"To be or not to be."

To love life will often be a victory over death or the taste for nothingness. To abandon the test or hold good until the end, that is the challenge. Endurance begets patience and patience is victory in the test (cf. Rm 5:3-4).

2 If the road is monotonous and gray
Take pleasure then in walking;
If your peace, as you go, amazes you
You will know the happiness of seeking.

As soon as you exist you are on your way. And from your beginning you obey, because you were not there to choose and decide if you wanted to be or not to be. Homo viator—*man on his way—even defines you. Created, you are a creature, and consequently dependent on a Creator who wanted you from all eternity as a beloved being.*

Every road means walking and requires your agreement, but this consent will constantly require a motive, which often will not be evident. In obscurity, in doubt, fear or anguish when faced with the unknown, you will often have to reduce your only ambition to courage to live, and dimly find in it a kind of pleasure. It is in this fidelity and this faith that peace will be given to you, or rather, that you will receive peace as you go along. You will know that to seek God is to discover Him.

As an ancient monk said about the disciples of Emmaus and their astonishment when they were walking along at the Lord's side: Eundo crescat affectus; *that is, it is as one goes along that ardor increases. Yes, you will know the happiness of seeking. Christ* is *the Way. As soon as you are on the way you have found Him, and at the same time, in Him, Truth and Life. You will know that in Him—in the pleasure of seeking Him unceasingly—will be your life and truth. He will show you what you will have to suffer, but your heart will be burning on the way (cf. Lk 24).*

3 To seek in your deepest self
(And it is exactly that, the test)
Him alone more yourself than you
To love him by giving him proofs.

The happiness of seeking, of seeking happiness . . . Would to seek no longer not be to despair? The life of the spirit is perhaps identical to the blessed uneasiness which keeps us watchful; holy curiosity, whose opposite is satiety, sluggishness and boredom. Seeking has no end because once we have been attracted the quest knows no limits. Still, the universal is never reached by extension but rather by depth. What is deepest is what is interior. Saint Augustine expressed this so very well when he said that you will not find (what you seek) outside yourself, but in what is inmost. The test of conscience, then, consists in its return to itself. Knowledge of self is possible only on condition of withdrawing our conscience from dispersion and daily distractions so that it may recollect itself at this absolute point where it can reach out and open up to the One, who is more itself than it is itself. Thanks to this meeting—like when a person meets someone he or she loves—the soul becomes free and happy; it loves itself and loves . . . A spontaneous expression of a sentiment of gratitude which seeks to share what it has received bears witness to this love. The test of loving is to experience its challenge. It is to will to love, to will to give proof of loving, even—and perhaps especially—when one recognizes one's unworthiness and poverty. And is this not always the case? "To love is to depend" (Paul Valéry). True love is an action: to want to be dependent and not to dominate.

4 Now, there is no other proof of loving
But love: "I love because I love."
They will make but one, lover and loved
Only when drawn into this love supreme.

Loving is an act so disinterested that it has no other intention. For a man or woman who loves, nothing but love can be the proof or reason for it. That was what Saint Bernard thought: "I love because I love, I love to love." (SC 83.4) Thus, when it comes to convincing the beloved the lover will not find any other proof as evident as his or her sentiment. He or she will not hunt for words or signs. A fortiori, *when it comes to God who is Love, a proof would be just as useless as it is impossible, because it would not add anything to what is evident. "Lord, you know everything, you know that I love you" (Jn 21:17). One can of course want to give signs of love, such as a kiss, but they will never be anything but manifestations of an interior reality, not proofs in the usual sense of the word. In a certain way, the proofs of God make it seem as if one doubts Him. Everyone knows that proofs cannot prove anything at all. The gratuitousness of loving is the sign of its absolute nature and is also its secret.*

As to the two lines which follow: "They will make but one . . ." Saint Augustine helps us to grasp their meaning by this beautiful passage:

> So that you may be able to have a foretaste of God, know that God is love, this love by which we love. Let no one say: "I do not know what I am to love." Let him love his brother and he will love Love itself, because in reality one knows the love whereby one loves better than one knows one's brother himself. God can be more known to him than his brother, really more known because more present.[12]

Swept up into divine Love, human love experiences unity comparable to that of the Trinity and reflects its clearness in charity. I love by Love itself. Even the presence of Love is closer, more certain than love of one's neighbor. Levinas well expressed this mystery of divine otherness in one phrase when he wrote: "When a person experiences presence it is not the person who experiences it, it is God who experiences the person. The person experiences that he is experienced."[13] *This is the true meaning of "life as a test," which explains why Gabriel Marcel's discovery of it led him to faith. In its reality, life requires the presence of the Creator who "tests" his creature. The double meaning of the word "test" is also the double meaning of the verb "love," which is then identified with the real presence of one's neighbor or of the One in me who is more me than I myself am.*

5 Love bears the test of time
To find it is to seek it unceasingly,

12. Saint Augustine, *De Trinitate,* Book VIII, ch. 8, §12. PL 42: 957–958.
13. Emmanuel Levinas, *Hors sujet,* 110.

To wait for it, grasp it for an instant
To remember it, so it will reappear.

No matter how perfect it may be, the love by which we love undergoes the test of time because life is a test, not in the sense that it is punishment or chastisement but that it is simply the challenge of our temporal condition, a contest we must face up to like a test to pass. The following three lines give us its modalities, the means of "passing time" and of overcoming the obstacle it presents to our freedom to love. To seek it, Saint Bernard said, is to love it because one cannot seek love without having found it already. So to seek it unceasingly means that we can never drop out of the race; it means staying awake in Time with its past, present and future solicitations, conscious that remembering supports us as we wait. Love is eternal in time and can be grasped in time only in passing.

Love cannot do otherwise than prevail over the trial of time which is ultimately death. Love is as strong as death and time; it is eternity. "Your love is everlasting!" (Ps 135). A person's whole life is the experience of this combat between love and time, which threatens life with old age and death. That is true of spiritual love just as it is of love subject to time. We often need a great deal of patience, but patience and length of time accomplish more than force or rage.

6 Sometimes life is like sleep
Peopled by nightmares or dreams
A night to ripen an awakening
Eternal, which will make it seem to us brief.

Sleep, necessary for life, is our daily experience of our temporal finite state. It is the symbol of death. Our whole life, whether we are awake or asleep, is sometimes and for long periods like a night of the senses or of the soul. Even in its mystical states the life of faith knows and experiences this kind of fall of tension or pressure (depression). Dreams or nightmares invade our powerless subconsciousness. The soul is then at the mercy of a sort of double of itself. It can even happen that it lives in a way that is different from the state of wakefulness, and by its suffering it may acquire greater maturity. In this way life in the body is a time of growth during which the soul matures so that it becomes capable of the eternal, like an embryo in its mother's womb. Sleep and night are thus symbolic parallels of time and eternity. Death is then no longer anything but an awakening, a reawakening which will make our earthly life seem like time during which we have been waiting for daybreak. When we think of it this way, the destiny of a created being is revealed to be an immensely disproportionate reality. A moment of trial for an eternity of blessedness. In this contrast each person can find graces of patience and ardent hope.

7 The test is to wait infinitely
Until to all who love it is revealed
This love which ardently waits
To reveal them all to themselves.

The first line of this stanza, like the first line of the following one, express the same experience because "to wait for" is at the same time both a test and happiness. Two texts by Gabriel Marcel which say this quite clearly come to my mind. I have meditated them so often that they certainly must have inspired these two lines, even though I was not thinking about them at all when I wrote them. They are the following: "To love someone is to expect something undefinable from him; at the same time it is to give him in some way the means of replying to this expectation."[14]

And the second quotation brings out the test of waiting: "One could even say that love, far from merely implying the acceptance of risk, in a certain way requires it. It is as though it calls for a kind of testing from which it comes out triumphant (the winner)"[15]

The grace of poetry is to be able to say everything, even what cannot be said, without ever having to state things with precision.

14. Gabriel Marcel, *Homo Viator* (Paris: Aubier, 1944 [new edition 1963]) 63. English edition (Chicago: Henry Regnery, 1951).

15. Gabriel Marcel, *La dignité humaine* (Paris: Aubier, 1964) 103.

I wrote this phrase at a time when I was thinking about giving up writing poems. Why did I want to justify this in prose? Perhaps because these two ways of expression are blended together and merge with the experience of age . . . My poem of only thirty-six lines can be read in ten minutes, for thirty thousand days of life . . .

8 Desire is the happiness of waiting
And peace, to be loved and loving.
The fire must remain fire under the ashes
And patiently consume you.

In these two stanzas it seems to me that the gift of grace which reveals us to ourselves by revealing itself to us is expressed. This divine love is also waiting ardently to be able to penetrate the soul, which should let it enter freely.

All the parables of the Kingdom speak of this vigilant, persevering, patient waiting. The one that is most expressive because it speaks of a revealing experience is that of the woman about to give birth. She suffers, but scarcely has she brought forth the child when she immediately forgets her trial because of her joy to have brought a human being into the world. Life thought of as a test has no better symbol than this new birth. "Desire (for God) is the happiness of waiting (for Him)," it is also the peace that comes from the discovery of a meaning to life and love.

This fire, which in youth is the symbol of victorious and ardent life, will remain in the embers of old age if the dry wood patiently consents to letting itself be consumed.

9 And when your bodily death will come
At the close of this road which ends,
Let the immortal soul escape it
And go on to love infinitely.

At the close of this road which is ending, I notice that I have written on page 53 of my memoirs[16] *that the truest image of a lifetime is a road followed until the end. I continue to think that*

16. Unpublished.

this is a very beautiful image, a very realistic one, and I ask myself if this does not come from memories of my childhood and youth, when I was a Boy Scout and cyclist and read Fr. Joseph Folliet's beautiful book entitled La Spiritualité de la route. *In any case, it is an image which has often come to my mind during my life: a road, a path to be travelled. I already mentioned this same image in the first stanza of this poem. Death then is the end of the road, and I think that we can think of it as the end of the test which life is.*

The title of the poem: "The Test of Loving" has intrigued certain readers and has not always been understood. I have received various commentaries. An Irish confrere sent me Job's words: "Is man's life on earth nothing more than pressed service, his time no better than hired drudgery?" (Job 7:1). I had not thought of that at all, but obviously that is the meaning of life, or at any rate, that is the experience of life. Still, the test is not to be thought of as a punishment but, on the contrary, in the sense that Saint Paul meant: "I am racing for the finish, for the prize" (Ph 3:14), or "All the runners at the stadium are trying to win, but only one of them gets the prize. You must run in the same way, meaning to win" (1 Co 9:24). This is how we should understand the test of life, and love is seen as an experience in this life which then is a race toward a goal; tenacity, courage, perseverance, as we find it in the New Testament. So it is in this sense that life advances toward a goal. Death then becomes the end of the test; but it is the end of a test that is like the end of a combat, reaching the end of the race with the angels and God applauding.

So death can be considered not as a goal or the end of everything, but as the termination of an Olympian test which then obviously ends in victory. Just recently I was reading a commentary on Scripture in which death, according to Levinas, is considered as the possibility of what is impossible, that is to say a means of surpassing a life which is simply natural. Rosenweig (the Jewish philosopher who was Levinas' mentor) wrote a commentary on the sixth day of Creation. After creation of the human being, at the end of this sixth day which finally concludes the work of six days, God did not say: "it is good" as he did on the preceding days, but he said that it was "very good." Rosenweig comments on the words "very good," saying that this is a prediction and that this "very good" of God's creation, or of the end of creation, of his work of creation, is death. This may surprise us; it is a bit like a kind of Jewish humor. Levinas picked this up and said that to reach God's rest, the Sabbath, this miracle of a kind of superior life is necessary, a supernatural life which can come about only by the end of time, or by the end of mortal time, the end of human, earthly time, to open out on true life; in Christian terms immortal life, eternal life.

I was deep in my thoughts on death when I received the death notice of one of my friends. When we were very young we went to school together and we were also members of the same scout troop. He was several years younger than I: he was twelve when I was sixteen. It is strange and a bit mysterious that I never forgot him, even though I never saw him again and never had any contact with him. All my life I have thought of him, wanted to see him again, and almost dreamt about him. It is very strange. Now I read in his death notice something stated quite simply which goes a little in the same sense as these meditations on the philosopher Levinas which I have just jotted down. "Fortunately, dying exists. If there were no death, there would be no hope, and if there were no hope, would life still have a meaning? Fortunately life ends on hope, fortunately dying exists." I find this a very beautiful commentary by a man who was totally contemporary, a father—even a grandfather—expressing his faith perfectly. And in the same death notice: "I believe that until the moment of my death I will remain a child." I do not believe that those who have read my memoirs can have missed seeing that this thought has come up again and again throughout my whole text, all through my life, as was the case with Rilke or Bernanos. Perhaps this sense of spiritual childhood may truly be the most beautiful image of the end of life, the end of the race and of hope, like a child, like a child of God. So the preceding are a few thoughts on the first two lines of this stanza. They express entirely the same idea:

Let the immortal soul escape it / And go on to love infinitely!

Obviously this infinite is truly the goal of finite existence. In-finite, non finite, leaving the finite, exiting temporal finite existence. I remember having written in a letter when I was twenty years old that man is not made for the absolute but contents himself, or ought to content himself, with a continual unstable balance. Now, as I think back over that part of my life, I think that the human being is meant for the absolute but that this absolute is not of this world; perfection is not of this world. This axiom and way of speaking can very well have a theological correlative; man is not made to enjoy beatitude or perfection here below. When I expressed this thought that man is not made for the absolute I of course meant to say that he is not made to live here below in the absolute. I think that it is a serious practical error into which we fall quite frequently (and into which I fell) to dream of living a fixed durable absolute here below in a continuous way. No, we live in hope. And I later rediscovered a passage in Fr. de Lubac's Paradoxes *which expresses this quite well:*

"Pilgrim of the Absolute *is a beautiful title, but we have to be careful to see that the first noun, as well as the second, keeps its exact value intact."*[17] *The first noun is* pilgrim, *and we are always pilgrims as long as we are traveling on this earth, in time. So then, the foregoing are a few reflections that can be made on the ninth and last stanza. Obviously, this absolute is the infinite; it is the infinity of death and it is thus that the wish of an immortal soul at the moment when it leaves mortal life is to be able to love infinitely.*

If the perfection of earthly life is to love, if it is charity, if it is love—as is attested by many people, by saints but also by very simple and just ordinary people like us,— often all that is worth remembering is what was love. That is what lives on from a life. What remains from an earthly life goes on to reach fulfillment at last in the infinite and to love infinitely.

17. Henri de Lubac, SJ, *Paradoxes* (Paris: Seuil, 1959) 97.

I do not know if the most beautiful wish, the most beautiful dream, or rather the most beautiful reality that our faith, our charity and our hope promise us is not to love infinitely.

* * *

Here I want to come back to several verses of my Chants *which express a little this experience which I have wanted to relate. While writing this poem I have come to realize that in wanting to comment on my poem I have actually said much less in the commentary than in the poem itself. It is an experience that I have made, but one could also say that the poem has expressed the experience of my life better than a hundred pages could have.*

Be that as it may, the verses of my Chants *that I am going to quote will perhaps—I could say undoubtedly—express still better the experience which I have wanted to transmit.*

> For the spirit life is a task to fulfill
> And the task is to love, whether one lives or dies,
> To explore in the given time the space of desire.
> (Chant V)[18]

And in the tenth Chant, *the last, where precisely I speak of my death:*

> These memories, these verses, all these fragments of a
> dream . . .
> The mystery of a life assembled in a vision . . .
> A continuous dream runs through our existence . . .
> From beginning to end, the joys and sufferings
> Were but allusions to the immense desire
> Which life and grace have turned into a single hope.
> (Chant X)[19]

. . . . *My hope, my immense and splendid hope!*

18. *Poèmes et Prières,* 74.
19. *Poèmes et Prières,* 83–84.

EPILOGUE

The "Test of Loving" was a high point in Fr. Charles' life as a monk-poet, but did not mean that he would stop writing. After decades of lecturing on Cistercian spirituality and the writings of the Cistercian Fathers, giving retreats in monastic communities, editing *Collectanea,* writing countless book reviews, numerous articles and poems, publishing his synthesis of Saint Bernard's spirituality—and all this in spite of frequent ill health—he continues to write both prose and poetry. Advancing in years, however, implies a different approach to life, a different view of life. His prose now consists chiefly of personal reflections on the spiritual life, on *his* spiritual life. In these recent writings one finds a bond with many authors whose works have nourished him throughout the years: the Cistercian Fathers first of all, especially St. Bernard and St. Aelred on whom his attention has been more particularly focused, but also a vast scope of authors of different epochs and cultures. He has likened the work of the monk's reading to the activity of a bee going from flower to flower, searching what can be turned into honey. So it is that the works of all those who seek the truth can be instruments in the monk's search for God. These drops of wisdom do not fall helter-skelter, but are assimilated into a vast picture. Throughout Fr. Charles' work he often comes back to the subject of memory—*memoria.* It is memory, one might say, which ties all the threads together and gives them their meaningfulness.

During the decades when Fr. Charles was going from monastery to monastery to give lectures on the Cistercian Fathers he took special interest in the young members of the Order, those in formation. He himself had been so favored at Scourmont by a novitiate under the guidance of Dom Anselme Le Bail and Fr. Albert Derzelle, that he wanted to communicate the same flame he had received to the young monks and nuns. He has succeeded in doing so.

Since Fr. Charles no longer gives lectures, a great deal of his time is given to meditation: on *The Song of Songs,* on *St. John's Gospel,* on familiar texts which have been a source of inspiration to him throughout the years and in the light of which he can see his own life. In spite of the fact that he had taken a resolution to write no more poems, others have come to him spontaneously—have been given to him, one might say— which go hand in hand with his spiritual life. Some of his more recent poems are composed of short verses, concise and meaningful, such as the following one written in 2002:

So little is needed

So little,
A small hope
Transforms
A remembrance.

A nothing
Moves me. A mystery
Of what is coming,
So empheral! . . .

So little is needed
To the hope, to the defiance
Of a departing soul . . .

There is a saying that a long life is a long grace. It can well be applied to this monk-poet, teacher and friend.

INDEX OF PERSONS AND PLACES

Since the name of Fr. Charles Dumont appears so frequently in the text, it is not included in this index.

*n = note